THIS IS WHERE IT ALL ENDS

From Broke Down To Boujee In 8 Unconventional Steps!

Troy Horne

Be sure to pick up the bonus material that goes with this book by visiting Thisiswhereitallends.com!

TABLE OF CONTENTS

INTRODUCTION

This book is for the outcasts, the overlooked, and the underrated. The world loves to bet against us. I know who you are and what you are made of. I'll take that bet. This book is for you. See you on the other side. – Troy Horne

There was a knock at the door. It was about 6 a.m. and I knew exactly who it was. I mean, I didn't actually know exactly who it was, but I had a good idea. I jumped out of bed because this brother was knocking like he was the po po about to do a home invasion or something. Plus, I was newly married and if it wasn't the police, I had a household to protect. Let's just say that I was "ret to distribute a healthy dose of these hands" if I needed to. I walked quickly to the door, looked through the peephole, and there on the other side of the door was a short stocky guy with a clipboard in his hand. He was wearing a white short sleeve mechanic's shirt with blue pinstripes. One of those joints with the sewn in name tags.

1

"What the hell?" I thought. "Who is it!" I barked back with that "I'm ret to go" bass tone in my voice. "Mr. Horne, it's Jeff Smith (not his real name) from Culver City Toyota. We're here to pick up your car Mr. Horne."

"Aww hell!" I thought. I knew that this moment was coming, but for some reason I was hoping that it wasn't actually going to happen. That evening I had called myself "preparing for this moment". I had parked in a tight parallel parking spot on the street so that it would be hard to get the car out with a tow truck. I called myself "thinking ahead." Apparently, "Jeff" was two steps ahead of me because he already had the car on the truck. Touché Jeff. Touché. I was living in the land of make believe right next to "denial river" and things weren't going as I had expected.

The land of make believe is where a lot of us live our entire lives. We pretend that life is better than it actually is. We get caught up on the "Only Positive Vibes" social media tour and "No Negativity" T-shirts. We refuse to talk about the bad stuff and as a result, do you know what happens? The problems build up and the bad stuff never goes away. In nine times out of ten, ignoring the bad stuff allows it to grow and become even more of a problem than it was in the beginning. You have to address the bad stuff, or it will come back to bite you in the ass.

Look no matter when or where you are reading this book, I need for you to know that this is it. This moment right here, is where all of the being passive about your life ends. This is where you start to live the life that you are supposed to be living.

There is a reason why you want more time with your family, less stress in your life, more money in your pocket, or whatever it is that you want. That reason is that somewhere deep down in your soul you know that's what you deserve. The problem has been that you were sold a bad bill of goods. You've been indoctrinated with all of the wrong ways to get to the more time, more happiness, and more money side of your life. We are going to change all of that within these pages. This is where it all ends and the you that you were meant to be begins. I can say that, because that is where I am right now. Plus, as you can see from the story that I started telling you, I know what it's like to be on the other side of this thing.

Think of it this way. As a missile heads toward its target, it constantly receives negative and positive feedback. If that missile was only receptive to positive feedback it would end up miles away from its target. But I guess, in the world of positivity only, it would hit the wrong target but feel really good about itself. Win win, right? WRONG! The unsuspecting target would not be happy. That's where you are right now. Time to get you back on track.

Could you imagine getting on a plane to go on vacation and getting off in a totally different place just because the pilot turned off all of the negative input from her navigation system. "No negativity! Only positivity!" she would say as you got off that Hawaiian-bound plane in New Jersey. Sounds fun right? Well, that's what the positivity only way of thinking is doing to people. That's what your current programming is doing to you. For those of you who are in the only negative feedback and say nothing when good things happen crowd, we'll get to you in a sec.

A lot of us live our lives afraid to face our problems. We know what our problems are, but instead of working to fix them we choose to look the other way and act like they aren't there. We go through life hoping things will get better and when they don't, we blame the thing for not fixing itself.

That was me in this story. I mean, I hadn't paid my car note for three months. What was I expecting? Oh, and like most of us I had plenty of "great" reasons why I hadn't paid my car note (at least I thought I did):

☐ I didn't have any money.

☐ I'd lost my job and I hadn't found another one yet.

☐ I was "trying." (Don't get me started on this one.)

☐ It was too expensive.

☐ The lease was super predatory.

By the way, none of those are great reasons, but they work really well for you if you are living in the land of make believe.

As Mel Robbins says in that viral video floating around the interwebs, "Nobody's coming to save you." You are the cavalry. Nobody cares about all of your excuses and great reasons why your shit ain't happening. Other people have their own excuses. They have their own great reasons for their own lives. This one is up to you to figure out.

Well, now it's up to me and you. If you feel stuck in your life and don't know how to take things to the next level this book is going to be where that stuckness ends. If you feel like your relationships aren't growing or you've lost your way in life, then you're in luck. This book is where that feeling ends. This is where it all ends. This is where your old way of living that has made you feel stuck, lost, and without purpose ends and your new next level life begins. I'm your Beyonce. Time for me to upgrade ya!

This is where we stop waiting for the rescue helicopter. It ain't coming. You are the one you that you're waiting for. You are it! You are the hero in your story. On top of all of that you are more than capable of saving yourself. You just gotta learn how. We are going to go over a different way of doing things. There is a different way of going through life and it works.

This book is going to show you how to do exactly that. I can't wait to hear how you leveled up your life once you got to the end of this book.

Oh, one more thing before we go on with the story. This book comes with a free download full of bonus materials. I couldn't put everything in the book. So, I put all of the videos and extra stuff in your bonus materials download. Think of it as your "How to upgrade your life the right way guide". It's a free gift from me to you. Go to thisiswhereitallends.com and download it right now. You are going to want that information. Go get it. NOW!

Also, if you're reading the paperback version of this story, go and get the audiobook version. There are some things I added in there that will help you too. Sometimes the inspiration hits and you can't make it make sense in print. It just doesn't have the same effect. So go and get the audiobook version if you have the print version, and if you have the audiobook version then go and get the print version. There are places to take notes in the print version and, as you will learn later in this book, writing things down is a super important and crucial part of your success.

OK, back to "Jeff" from Culver City Toyota.

"Why is he here?" Elizabeth asked as she walked to the door and stood behind me. At that moment she didn't know all of the stuff that I just told you. She didn't know that I hadn't paid my car note for the past three months. She didn't know that my money situation was bad (to say the least). We had just gotten married a couple of months before this wonderful incident and although we were married, we weren't quite at the point in our relationship where we were talking about the money stuff.

(Word of advice to all of you looking to get married: talk about the money stuff while you are dating. It's a part of your relationship and it's super important to the health of your marriage. For most of us talking about money is uncomfortable, but if you don't do it things will get a lot more uncomfortabler. Don't live in the land of make believe like I did.)

"They're here to pick up my car. I'm behind on my payments." I said like a kid who just got caught with his hand in the cookie jar for the tenth time. I was embarrassed as hell. I opened the door and there stood the repo guy, clipboard in hand. He looked at me, then at my wife, and then back at me. "We're here to pick up the car, Mr. Horne. Do you have the key?" he asked.

Brother was mad polite by the way. I guess you learn to read the room in the repo business. You probably don't want to start the interaction with a hostile tone if you don't have to. I'm sure this kind of thing can go from zero to a hundred real quick. #ohlawd

Despite his courteous demeanor, it still felt like I had just been drop kicked in the face by The Rock. However, we were not about to rumble or take anyone's face off. (See what I did there?) It was all that I could do to keep from breaking down in tears. I had never felt this level of failure before in my life.

Don't get me wrong, I had failed a lot before then. I had moved to Los Angeles and not made it yet as a musician. I had been dropped by my record label. My credit was wrecked, which was why I had signed that horrible car lease in the first place. #myfault

Yeah, I had failed a LOT before my car got repossessed, but none of them felt like this! Those other failures were all private failures. Only I had to deal with them. Now all those problems that I had tried to ignore were being put on display right in front of my wife!

Still, there I was the "man of the house" and I couldn't even pay my car bill. We ain't even gonna talk about the rent. I was out of work and my car was being repossessed in front of my wife at five in the morning. "The best part of waking up is LOSER in your cup." It was one of my lowest moments in life.

"No problem man. I'll be right back," I said as I went to get the car keys. When I came back, my wife was picking a fight with the guy. Can you imagine that? She was mad at him for doing his job and not at me for not paying my bill! We're not even going to talk about not telling her I was behind on my car note part. She's a real one, that Elizabeth. Love you sweetie.

"Do you guys ever get beat up?" I heard her ask the guy as I returned to the front door. The guy looked at me and I looked back at him with the "bro we ain't about to fight over this car" look. I was six feet tall, 195 pounds, and I looked like I was very familiar with the gym, because I was very familiar with the gym. I'm still six feet tall, just not 195 anymore. Don't judge me. Nevertheless, I wanted him to know that we were not about to throw down over a car repo.

"Sweetie, he's just doing his job," I said as I handed him the keys.

"This isn't fair," she insisted as he backed away, keeping his eyes on the both of us.

We walked back into the apartment and closed the door. At that point I was emotionally beyond done. I broke down and bawled like a little baby. I couldn't hold it in. I'm not the crying type, but that moment had me "tore up from the flo up!" Elizabeth sat with me and consoled me, which to be honest kind of blew my mind. I mean there I was, pretty much a deadbeat husband with no job who just had his car repossessed, and she was consoling me. To this day that still blows my mind. I pulled myself together and told her I was fine.

Then I pulled out the newspaper I had purchased for this job seeking thing and acted like I was getting back on the job search. Even back then, the jobs in the newspaper suuuucked! To top it off, I now had no car to go to an interview in. Elizabeth checked on me one last time and then went to get ready for work. I went back to feeling sorry for myself. After about forty-five minutes or so she left. After the door closed behind her, I really went in on the pity party of one!

I was bawling uncontrollably. I'm talking Viola Davis, nose running, lying down on the ground and howling uncontrollably kind of crying. I was crying so hard that I couldn't see anything. It was bad. I'd be lying if I said that I didn't think about suicide back then because I did. I thought of a lot of things that aren't necessarily the best things to think about when you're down. I was deep in my victimhood. I was super depressed, and I was doing the victim talk that a lot of us do when times get tough. Everything was everyone else's fault.

"The car payment was too high. Why would they charge that much for that car anyway?"

"I told them that I didn't have a job when I missed my first payment. Why wouldn't they just let me float for a little while? I've made all of my payments up until a few months ago."

"Why won't any of these jobs call me back?"

"My parents don't have enough money to help me out. It's their fault."

"Society is racist."

"School didn't prepare me for success. It barely prepared me to survive."

"I didn't have any mentors to guide me."

Blah Blah Blah. . . .

Were some of those things true? Maybe. But what I want you to understand is that it didn't matter if they were true or not!

No matter what your excuses are, your excuses don't matter. Mine didn't matter then and yours don't matter now. Either we're getting shit done or we're not. Here's why none of our excuses matter.

None of our excuses make our lives better.

We have all heard that life is short and that's because it is. We don't have time to focus our energy on anything that doesn't improve our lives or the lives of others. Excuses don't do that. They don't improve ANYTHING!

Our goal in this life should be to enjoy our lives and enjoyment comes from making our lives better. So that being said, NONE of our excuses matter. None of them.

What mattered in this specific situation was that I wasn't taking responsibility for my life. What matters above all else is that you are not taking responsibility for your life. I can guaran-got-damn-tee-it.

We are all guilty of playing the blame game: It's this person's fault. It's that person's fault. It's Amerikkka. It's this. It's that. Hey, I'm not saying that you don't have obstacles others don't have, but the thing that's stopping you is YOU! People became millionaires one generation out of slavery. (See Madam C.J. Walker) There's no way that anything you're facing today is more challenging than that. There is no way that you are facing more racism than that. There is no way that you are knocking your head against a glass ceiling lower than the one that she faced. There is no way. Take responsibility for where you are. It's not them. It's you!

At the end of the day, I was the one who signed that horrible lease. I was the one who didn't make the payments. I was the one who had allowed myself to be at the mercy of an employer. I was responsible then, and if anything goes sideways, I AM responsible now. I am always the one who is responsible for my life, and you are the one who is ALWAYS responsible for yours. Now, sometimes you get a helping hand during those moments of struggle. That day I got mine.

As I was lying on the floor bawling my eyes out about having my car repoed, I looked up. You know how they say that when the student is ready the teacher will appear? Well, the teacher appeared to me in that moment. Right in front of me, on the bottom shelf of our living room bookshelf was this red book spine. At least that's what it looked like. I do remember that it caught my eye and I also remember that it was like this bright beacon at the time. It was kind of weird. I crawled over to it because I was being super dramatic, and I took it off the shelf. The book title read *Think and Grow Rich.*

I was thinking, "Well, that sums up everything I need. If I can think and grow rich, I am in." I had never heard of this book before. I had never heard of self-help before. This whole idea about your thoughts creating your reality was brand new to me. I opened it up and there inside was a set of audio cassettes. Yup, you read that right audio cassettes. Like I said, it was back in the day. So, I took the first one out, put it in our tape player, and pressed play.

What happened next was an amazing journey into my own head trash. I realized, thanks to this tape/audiobook, that I had a LOT of trash up in there. Because of that book,

I realized that most of the things that I had been taught to believe were keeping me stuck in the same old grind of lack.

I had to get out of my own head in order to step into my new life. I was at rock bottom and trust me when I say that I wanted something new. That was the moment when it all began to end for me. The old self was put on notice and the new self was born. At that moment God, the universe, or whatever you call it, noticed ya boi sitting down in this little well and said, "Hey, here's a ladder if you want to climb out."

You see, when you hit rock bottom the only way out is up. Well, actually, that's not true. You can keep digging despite what people say. However, I wasn't interested in that option. The bottom sucked enough for me to decide that I didn't need any more of that. I was literally penniless, I didn't have a job or any income, and my car had just been repossessed. I'll take a different option for 100 Alex.

Are you ready for something different in your life? That's a question you have to ask yourself. That's an answer only you can give. Are you tired of the suck?

Funny story, I was at the airport recently and the line for a particular low fare airline was ridiculously long. I mean the line zigged and zagged down half of the terminal. People were clearly going to miss their flights. I wasn't on that airline thank goodness. I had learned earlier in life that cheap isn't really cheap. What I mean is, you are going to pay no matter what. You are either going to pay with your money or you are going to pay with your time. Either way, you are going to pay. Despite how much people love to say that they've saved money the only thing that is truly irreplaceable is time. They ain't making any more of that stuff.

Long story longer, I got checked in on my airline and went to the bathroom before going through security. When I came out of the bathroom, the incredibly long line was even longer. It was no longer "I can't believe it" long. It was now "this is ridiculous" long.

I said excuse me as I crossed the crazy long line to go to security. As I came out on the other side, a little girl and her family walked in front of me on their way to security as well. Her little brother asked what the line was for. She told him that it was for this "low fare airline", not saying their name because I don't want to get fined. He responded with something like, "Wow. That's not good." To which she ended the conversation with, "It sucks to suck." In that moment, that girl was my spirit animal! She was 100% right. It sucks to suck.

I've seen people who hit the bottom and kept digging and it ain't pretty. Hell, I've been one of them multiple times in my life. However, this time was different. This time was the lowest of the low moments in my life and I was no longer interested in digging down. This time I knew that it sucked to suck.

Think and *Grow Rich* was the book that made me say, "This is where it all ends!" It was the first book that made me think about what was going on in my life. It was the first book to show me how to change it.

My hope is that this book will be that for you. Thanks to Napoleon Hill I got to see that I was hoarding thoughts and opinions that I had received from other people and 99.9% of those thoughts were self-defeating and limiting. You are probably doing the same thing and that's why you picked up this book.

Well, buckle up buttercup, because "It's about to go down." Your life is about to change and change for the better.

The first thing you have to realize is that most of your own head trash has nothing to do with you. Most of your head trash was dropped off on the streets of your mind by someone else. Most of the time it was put there under the disguise of concern and care. Now before you go getting mad at your mom, dad, auntie, uncle, cousin, or friend for being a "hater," remember that it's not their fault.

"My uncle told me that I'd never sell a million records. I sold a million records like a million times." – JAY-Z

Remember that someone did it to them first. They didn't just start hating on you because you're something special. Someone deposited that head trash into their thoughts, and they were just passing along the family heirloom. Don't hate the player. Hate the game. Oh, and stop passing along head trash. Real talk.

That being said, it doesn't matter why or how those self-limiting thoughts got into your head. All that matters is that you take them out. No recycling necessary.

By the end of this book, you will not only have the success mindset you need to get rid of all that limiting belief stuff; You will also have an action plan on how to move forward toward living the life you dream about.

Will it be easy? No. But it will be worth it. So, let's get started. Now, I want you to know that this book isn't for everyone. Some people aren't built for this and if that's you then you should know before you spend one more minute reading. So, let's find out if this book is for you or if this book is NOT for you.

This Book Is Not For You If...

Keeping it 100 is going to rub you the wrong way. You know what? Let's get all of the pleasantries out of the way right here and now.

Pleasantry number one. I don't do pleasantries. In this book, I'm not going to sugar coat anything. I've tried to do the sugar-coating thing in the past and it's just not me. So if you need to feel good all the time or if you need somebody to pump you up before they tell you the truth about why things aren't going the way you want them to go, then you're reading the wrong book.

Put it down or send it back to wherever you bought it from because this isn't the book for you. Pick up something that does the "always look on the bright side" stuff, because this journey won't be that.

This book is for people who are tired of the rosey feel good bullshit that doesn't do anything to help you actually improve your life. This book is for the people who are ready to make actual change in their lives and that, my friend, doesn't always feel good. #inthebeginning

Pleasantry number two. I am a southern 80's kid. This book will be from that perspective. If the last few years have shown us anything, it's that there are definitely different experiences on the planet. This book will be written from my experience. If the use of slang or any of that stuff is going to bother you, then you're reading the wrong book. Put it down or send it back to wherever you bought it from. Ya' welcome.

Pleasantry number three. There will be work to do. I'm not going to babysit you and make sure that you do the work. This book will tell you what work you need to do. In a couple of cases it will even show you how to do it, but it won't make you do it. You're going to have to find it in yourself to get it done. In this game, it's you vs. you, and self-mastery is something you have to choose for YOURSELF. Results from this book will vary based on your commitment to yourself.

In this book I am going to share with you all of the steps that I took and all of the exercises and tools that I used to get where I am today. When I did this stuff, I found myself waking up to the life that I had dreamed about. Anything that I can do, you can do too. The question is, will you?

Finally, just to wrap up the repo story before we move on. Things did end up working out. After this low point of having my car repossessed, I went on to:

- [ ] Grow one of my businesses from 0 to multiple six figures a year.

- [ ] Start a side hustle that made me an extra $74,020.08 a year on top of that business.

- [ ] Raise a beautiful family with my wife.

- [ ] I'm able to spend time with them every day.

- [ ] I don't wake up to an alarm clock and haven't for about ten years.

☐ And a lot more. . . .

I share this with you only to show you that no matter where you are right now it can and does get better when you change your mindset. I'm still not where I want to be, but I ain't where I used to be and for me that's huge. Change your thoughts change your life.

Do you want to wake up living the life of your dreams? Do you want more overall happiness, peace, and love in your life? Do you want your time back? Well, then keep reading. We have a LOT of work to do, but it's definitely going to be worth doing.

That being said, my lawyer will kill me if I don't tell you this disclaimer so here it goes. *I cannot guarantee that you will have the same results that I have had.* I don't know your work ethic and I don't know how dedicated you are and a lot of other stuff. What I can guarantee is that you will have the blueprint. What you do with it will be up to you. No guarantees, but all the instruction is coming your way. (My lawyer is happy now.)

Yup, as a result of getting out of my own head I was able to make more money so that the repo thing would never happen to me again. I was able to spend more time at home with my family like I dreamed of doing when I was a kid. I'm basically a stay-at-home dad these days, and I was able to help my kids pursue their dreams, both mentally and financially.

More importantly than all of that, I was able to be at peace with this thing called life. I was able to be at peace with myself. That last one is more important than all the other stuff. Peace of mind is priceless! Peace with yourself is pricelesser!

Let's jump in. We have so much work to do. Thank you for allowing me to be a small part of your journey. I look forward to hearing about your success. Now let's get on with step 1.

CHAPTER 1

STEP 1–THE ULTIMATE GAME CHANGER

The absolutely positively first thing that you must do is take responsibility for everything in your life.

I was going to start this section off with some fun story or anecdote, but I figured I'd keep it simple and get straight to the point. Sometimes you need the medicine without the spoon full of sugar. #sorrymarypoppins but it be's that way sometimes.

Let me say it again: you have to take responsibility for everything that happens in your life from here on out. If things go well, take responsibility. If things go poorly, take responsibility. If things just go. Take responsibility. Take responsibility for everything that happens in your life. As Snoop Dogg said in his walk of fame acceptance speech:

Last but not least, I wanna thank me

I wanna thank me for believing in me. I wanna thank me for doing all this hard work.

I wanna thank me for having no days off

I wanna thank me for, for never quitting.

I wanna thank me for always being a giver, and tryna give more than I receive.

I wanna thank me for tryna do more right than wrong.

I wanna thank me for just being me at all times.

Snoop Dogg, you a bad motherfucker. – Snoop Dogg

The first time that I heard the idea of taking responsibility for everything, my first thought was "What? I'm responsible? That can't be right. I must have heard that wrong." I had to, as Kanye puts it, "Stop and rewiiiind that!" I had never heard of this before.

In my life as a young adult there was always someone or something to blame when things went wrong. Society was doing this to me. This person was doing that to me. That person was doing this to me. The devil was trying to trip me up. I could always find someone to blame for my bad days and poor outcomes when I was younger.

However, as you saw, that led to a life of repossessed cars, bad credit, and an overall bad financial situation that could have turned into a bad relationship situation. Finances are the number one cause of relationship stress. I was right on course. I needed to take responsibility for that and for everything that was happening in my life. At the time I wasn't doing that. As one of my favorite virtual mentors Jim Rohn says:

"Take full responsibility for what happens to you. It's one of the highest forms of human maturity. Accepting full responsibility. It's the day you know you've passed from childhood to adulthood. The day you accept full responsibility." – Jim Rohn

Taking responsibility for everything is the biggest gift you can give yourself. If all those mental conversations that you have with yourself begin and end with, "Well, it's my fault. I'm responsible." The head chatter ends a lot faster. All that back and forth that you used to do about this possibility and that possibility end real quick. You become a lot more focused on how to either fix the problem or keep it moving. There really isn't much to talk about outside of that when the conversation starts with, "It's my fault."

On the flip side of that. Some things you can control and some things you can't. You still have to take responsibility for everything, but you also have to know which is which. In things you can't control, you're responsible for how you respond to the situation.

Wayne Dyer said this:

"If you can control it don't worry about it because you can control it. If you can't control it don't worry about it because you can't control it."

– Wayne Dyer

I'm going to write that one more time so that you have to read it one more time. Wayne Dyer once said some of the truest stuff you will ever hear.

"If you can control it don't worry about it because you can control it. If you can't control it don't worry about it because you can't control it."

Taking responsibility for everything in your life puts you in a space to evaluate everything that comes in and everything that goes out. If you can control it, then you go and take care of it. If you can't control it, then you let go and don't worry about it.

The first question should always be, "Can I control this?" If the answer is yes, then ask yourself, what can you do to make it better? If the answer is "No, I can't control this," then the conversation is over and you move on with your life.

There goes about half of your head trash conversations right there...

This Dude Sounds Like My Mom

The first time I heard Jim Rohn I knew that I had found my guy. Like my mom, Jim Rohn had zero tolerance for the sob stories and excuses. Crying over spilled milk didn't clean it up.

In the first speech I heard from Mr. Rohn he went on to say ...

"I hope you'll understand that it's in your best interest to take responsibility for everything you do, but that's only the beginning. I'm also going to suggest that many times it's even best to accept responsibility for the mistakes of others." He goes on to say..."I can hear you saying..."What accept responsibility for someone else's mess ups? Why would I want to do something like that? Well, that's a fair enough question and over the next few minutes I'll try to answer it." – Jim Rohn

I'll put a link to the entire speech over on the free download that comes with this book. It's a great speech and you should hear him say it. It's a lot better than me typing it. Go to *thisiswhereitallends.com* and get it. It's free and it will help you out a lot!

Up until that moment I had a sliding scale of responsibility. The easy things were my fault. I mean, I could handle those problems and failures being my fault. They weren't a big deal. Everything else, all of that hard stuff, now that was someone else's fault. All of the big failures were "their" fault. Yeah, whatever you do. Don't be that guy. Be like Snoop. Take responsibility for everything.

From this point forward you have to learn to take responsibility for everything that happens to, for, because of, and in spite of you.

Now, that being said, don't go out into the world proclaiming your greatness when you win or your failure when you lose. This is an inside job. This is something that you are doing for you. This is something that happens inside your head but reflects out onto and throughout your life.

Taking responsibility for everything that happens in your life changes your internal conversation and we have a lot of those inside your head conversations. We all talk to ourselves more than we talk to anyone else in our lives. At least I do. I talk to myself 24/7. I never shut up! The great thing about taking responsibility for everything is that just by doing this one little thing, you become your own motivational speaker. It's the most empowering thing that you will ever do in your life. I want to encourage you to keep this step to yourself in the beginning. As a matter of fact, I'm going to highly recommend it. And when I say highly, I mean highly!

Most of the people that you know will not understand your new "take responsibility for everything' mentality. If you share what you are doing too early in your process a lot of the people around you will try to pull you back into the old blame game. Keep this process to yourself. What happens in this book stays in the book. I'm being serious. At least in the beginning. Right now, your job is to fix you first. Like the flight attendant says, "Place your oxygen mask on first before helping others." Do that. Your job is to move YOU to a new paradigm. Your job is to fix you first. Your job is to take responsibility for it all starting now!

This has not only been life changing for me, it has been life changing for my marriage. Despite Elizabeth and I being on the same page (for the most part ☺) I've realized that we're doing this life thing "together alone". By that I mean, we are here together, but our journeys are ours and ours alone.

When I decided to take responsibility for my life it became really hard to be mad at her for anything. I mean, if I wanted something to happen, then it was my responsibility to make it happen. If I wanted something I needed to get off my ass and go get it. In the past, I would've blamed her.

This: "Why doesn't she do the dishes right now? The sink is piling up."

Changed to this: "Why don't you get off your ass and do the dishes right now yourself? The sink is piling up."

In that moment, I was the one that was bothered by it, so I was the one who needed to fix it. Now, I am going to need for you to use some of your discernment and not be a complete idiot. Obviously, there are things that you just can't go off and do if you are in a relationship, but those are few and far between. The little things are usually what cause the big issues in relationships. Taking responsibility for those little things usually gets rid of the animosity buildup that happens over time.

If you want it done, then get up and get it done.

You are responsible.

The Marriage Whisperer and The Cash

It was the beginning of 2020. Our business numbers were good, but they weren't great. Elizabeth and I had just had our seasonal tiff about money and business and systems. I was still blaming her for this and that and I'm sure she was over it. We just do business differently.

She was uncomfortable and I was uncomfortable, and we were fighting because of it. In this particular case, I was wanting to charge one of our clients for being late on their payments. (Oh the irony.) Our established system said that after the fifth of the month your payment was late and the consequence for being late was getting charged a late fee.

I was in charge of emailing people and collecting the late fee, so in my mind I was taking responsibility for something that drove me crazy. I would email them pretty much every day after the first with a link so they could process their payment. In my opinion, a daily reminder for something was more than enough.

However, for probably the tenth or eleventh time that year, someone was late on their payment and in addition to being late they were protesting the late fee. I mean, I get it. Who likes paying a late fee? But for me it was a case of not taking responsibility. Don't like paying a late fee? Don't be late.

Now mind you I was emailing them every day and saying, please pay now to avoid the late fee, and they were not responding to any of my messages, but hey whatevs. The day before the late fee was charged, I would even send an email that said something like, avoid the late fee by processing your payment today or something like that.

However, Elizabeth is a nicey nice. Remember she got mad at the repo guy back in the day. So, you can imagine how she fought for those clients when they didn't want to pay the late fee. Long story still going, someone had complained about being charged a late fee and she was taking their side. I'd had it.

This had been a thing for a while, and I just didn't want to keep having this same argument every month. So, what did I do? I said, do you know what sweetie? You seem passionate about not charging this late fee and I'm pretty passionate about charging a late fee. So, I am going to step away and let you manage the entire business. I'm going to start another business and that way you can have your thing and I can have mine and we don't have to keep having this issue every month.

In that moment I took responsibility for my mental frustration. Had we built this business together? Yes. Had we struggled to make this thing work for years? Yes. Did I feel a little resentment that I had to step back from a business that I helped build? Yes. But I realized that I could do it again if I wanted to. I realized that our relationship was more important than this recurring issue. I realized that my mental health was more important to me than a late fee and that the easiest way to take care of myself in that moment was not to continue those monthly fights. The more responsible option was to step back and, as T-Pain said, "Do something else!"

I started looking into online businesses that I could start by myself for myself. It had to have a low startup cost and a high margin of profitability. Easy enough, right?

Then the pandemic hit and everything went crazy. I knew that we would have to tighten our money belts, but I would not let that stop me from moving forward with this new business. I was responsible for my future and that was all of the fire that I needed. Oddly enough, the shutdown that came with the pandemic made my new business grow even faster than it would have normally. Everyone was ordering stuff online and my business took off. Taking responsibility had paid off once again. It always has and it always will.

Now, I have a thriving online business and we don't have those frustrating conversations about late fees anymore. Our income has grown, I don't have to be unhappy when someone is late on their payments, and we have more streams of income and more time together. Did I mention more time together? Time freedom is the real power play. On top of that, we both get to do things our way. I took responsibility for that part of my life and because of it I now have my own soon to be multiple six figure business that I get to run any damn way that I choose! That, my friend, is what happens when you take responsibility. Marriage and relationship counseling session ovah!

Look, taking responsibility is a cheat code. Will it be easy? No, but nothing in life worth having ever is. Put your head down. Take responsibility for everything and get to work.

The best way to get out of your way mentally is to be like Jesus and take the wheel. Ya welcome! ☺

Your First Assignment

Time to be like Cardi B and understand the assignment. Your first assignment is to write down five bad things you're responsible for and five good things you're responsible for.

5 bad things that I am responsible for that didn't go the way I wanted.

---

5 good things that I am responsible for that went exactly the way I wanted.

Now look at anything you want to change on your lists and ask yourself the following:

Can I control that? Y/N

If the answer is yes, write down how you are going to change or improve it.

_____

_____

_____

_____

_____

_____

If the answer is NO. Let it go and move on with your life.

CHAPTER 2

STEP 2 – TALK TO YOURSELF LIKE YOU'RE ALL YOU GOT...'CAUSE...

W e all say things to ourselves that we would never say to our worst enemy. Am I right or am I right? If someone else said half of the things that we say to ourselves to ourselves, we would not be their friend. In some cases, we might even ask them to step outside to handle it. You have to change that. You have to go from being your worst enemy to being your best friend. You have to start talking to yourself like you're all you got because YOU ARE ALL THAT YOU GOT!

I used to talk to myself so bad that at one time I was considering suicide. The funny not so funny thing is that I negative self-talked myself out of it. That voice that had been dogging me pretty much all my life said one of the most powerful things I had ever heard. That voice said, and I quote, "If you kill yourself, I'm still going to be here."

Well, if that ain't a bitch. The voice that was tearing me down wasn't going anywhere no matter what I did. It was me. The voice that I was trying to escape was a permanent fixture in my life. It was like Diddy singing...

We ain't going nowhere...

We ain't going nowhere...

We can't be stopped now

Cause it's bad voice for life.

Well, now that I knew that little piece of information, I knew that I had to learn how to change that thang because that voice inside my head wasn't going anywhere. Dying wasn't even an option because that voice was going to be there too. For me, the problems outside at the time were hard, but that voice inside my head was the real ass kicker. Do you want to know what I did? I committed to kicking its ass and changing it into something that works for me instead of against me.

"When there is no enemy within, the enemy outside can do you no harm."

- African Proverb

Basically, it was me vs. me and there was no escaping this fight. There was no running or hiding from this one. This one was going to go down no matter what. There's something about knowing your back is up against the wall and there ain't no way out but through. That way of thinking makes you throw caution to the wind and come out swinging. That kind of situation usually results in creating champions. When there is no plan B you tend to find a way to make plan A work.

I set out to conquer that enemy and make it work for me. Since there was no retreat, that's exactly what I did. I laid out the steps that I took so that you can do it too. Here they are in all of their glory. Enjoy...

Step 1: Challenge

The first step in the process is to challenge that voice. If it says you can't do this or that, then ask it why not? Ask that voice, why is this person who did it better than me? Why are they more worthy or more capable than I am? Challenge that voice and keep challenging it. When I started doing the challenge thing that voice had all the answers.

"Yeah. . . . They are better than you," that voice would say. "Yeah, they are more worthy or more capable than you are." But then I'd remember that it was me vs. me. That's when that good angel on the other shoulder started to chime in. It started defending me. It would say, "Screw you, bad voice bro! No they aren't."

The other me got tired of the bullshit talk from the bad voice me. Your other "you" is asleep right now that's all. We need to wake up that other you.

Time to wake up the voice that told little Marquis to eat rocks when he said that your G.I. Joe collection sucked. Time to bring back the old you that once said, "I know you are but what am I?" when you were in the third grade. We need to bring that guy back. He's in there. He's just been quiet for a long time. Time to let him back out.

It all starts with challenging that voice that has gained dominance in your head. It all starts with asking, "Why not me?" F that other dude! It's time for him to shut up!

Step 2: Replace

Start replacing your negative talk with positive talk. Start saying nice things about yourself. A lot of other people will have a lot of negative things to say about you. Don't you be one of those people. Plus, all the negative things they have to say about you have zero to do with you and 100 to do with them.

Let me explain what I mean. You see, a lot of people don't want you to outshine them and it's not because of the reasons we all think. It has nothing to do with jealousy and everything to do with the lies they've been telling themselves. They are basically defending their own head trash against your over achiever ideology.

If you come along and reach your goals from the same life situation they're in, then the problem isn't the world, the problem isn't society or opportunity. The problem is them and ain't nobody who hasn't read this book got time for that! You reach success and the glaring truth will be staring them right in their face. It will be obvious that the problem is them and that's a hard pill to swallow. After you start to challenge negative talk Nancy you need to replace her with positive talk Patrice. It takes very little energy to say something nice to yourself so do it and do it every day!

As a matter of fact, here is a quick win exercise that I used that helped me a lot. Quick win for the books.

Go to the mirror right now!

Look at yourself and say, "I love you."

The first time I did it I cried like a baby. As you will see throughout this book ya boi is a baby. I'm cool with it though. The crazy thing is, we all go to the mirror and wash our face, brush our teeth, and comb our hair hopefully. You know what we don't do? We don't ever look at ourselves in the mirror, make eye contact and then follow that up with a big ol I love you!

Your second assignment is to do that every morning until the voice inside your head says, "I know!" It will change your life. Replace your negative self-talk with positive self-talk. Start with looking at yourself in the mirror every day and telling yourself that you love you!

Step 3: Remove

Remove all doubt by learning about the people who did what you want to do. The best thing you can do is to research your heroes. When you do this one simple thing, you'll find out that all of those super star people are just regular people.

In my life I have been able to meet a lot of famous people. It goes along with being a professional musician. It was a lot of fun. The great thing is that every time I meet one of those famous people, I realize that they're just like me. A lot of famous people just happened to be in the right place at the right time, or they kept going when other people gave up, or maybe they did the stuff that we are going to talk about in this book. Either way, I quickly learned that there is no magic to success. People are people and success has no favorites.

Your job in this section is to remove your self-doubt. Oh just remove self-doubt? Say less! I can hear you laughing, but stick with me. You are now about reaching your goal and the best way to do this is to learn about those who have gone before. When you read their biographies, auto or otherwise and learn their stories you will find that they are not better than you. They don't have some magic skill that you have t figure out. They put their pants on one leg at a time like everyone else. And that's about it. Learn how regular those people are that did what you want to do. That will shut the doubter inside your head right up.

I remember reading the Walt Disney biography because I want to be someone who changes people's lives through entertainment. (I have a dream of becoming an entertainment mogul one day, but that's neither here nor there.) I thought that this guy was the mark. I thought he had the magic touch and I had to figure out how to get. Until I read his biography. That's when I realized he was as regular as regular gets. No disrespect, but after that it was literally a case of "Anything You Can Do (I Can Do Better)."

Study the history of your industry. Learn about those who have gone before. It will change your life!

Step 4: Prove

Now go out there and prove it. You now have the tools to make it happen. You have the ability to make it happen, but you have the tell yourself that you're going to make it happen. No matter how many failures you have along the way you have to continue telling yourself that you'll be successful. You have to tell yourself that you are a winner and that you will win.

As you do the remove exercise and learn about other people who have been successful before you, you will learn about all of the failures they had to go through in order to reach their success. Your journey will be the same. Keep telling yourself that you are the best. Keep telling yourself that you are going to win. Keep talking positively to yourself about yourself.

Your words have amazing power. You have to talk to yourself positively all of the time.

You have to say great things about yourself over and over again. When you do this, those positive thoughts and words will become true. You will prove it if you speak it. Notice that I didn't say that you *might* prove it if you speak it. I said that you *will* prove it if you speak it.

The best way to get started is to set small goals. Everyone likes to set big goals and that is exactly what I tell you to do later in this book, but the key to large goals is a bunch of small steps. Set small steps and stack up a bunch of small wins. Do that and sooner rather than later you will find yourself looking at your big goal as the next small win in your journey.

Now to your homework for this section. Take a look at the next steps and make sure that you do them. There are only 8 assignments and each one is super important.

Your Second Assignment

List 5 negative things that you say to yourself that you are going to stop saying to yourself!

List 5 negative things that I will no longer say to myself.

_____

_____

_____

_____

_____

List 5 encouraging things I'm going to say to myself instead.

_____

_____

_____

_____

_____

List 3 people I am going to research.

_____

_____

_____

_____

_____

3 small wins that I am going to achieve first.

_____

_____

_____

_____

_____

CHAPTER 3

STEP 3 – STOP BEING AN HTH!

Every Saturday when I was a kid my sisters and I would go through the house and clean like there was no tomorrow. Not because we wanted to, but because Saturday was house cleaning day. That was what my mom had on the schedule and back then, we did what our parents told us to, no questions asked. Ha! I would go to sleep Friday night knowing that I was going to wake up to gospel music and the sound of a running vacuum. Those Saturday morning cleaning sessions were the bane of my existence . . . in the beginning. As I got older, they became my little Saturday morning walking meditations. I fell in love with cleaning! I learned how to scrub a toilet, dust furniture, and clean the grout of a shower stall until that shower stall looked brand new. I was a house cleaning pro and I loved it!

I got to the point where I loved the smell of Comet, Lemon Pledge, and Clorox in the morning. Those wonderful aromas were my jam. They still are if I'm being honest. I absolutely love cleaning the house to this day. It wasn't always like that though. In the beginning I hated it.

Despite my initial hatred for all things elbow grease, I wouldn't trade any of those weekends for the world. They were my first lessons in "do the hard work" because you deserve the results. Those weekends shaped my life for the better. However, you're gonna love the her-story behind those Saturday morning cleanings with mom. It's a pretty awesome little deal and it speaks to the power of my mom and her ability to turn every situation into something that works for her good. Here's the backstory on how cleaning became a thing in our household. My mom told me this when I asked her why we had to clean every weekend. Like to hear it? Here it go...

The Her-story Behind The Saturday Morning Gospel Cleans

It was 1968 in Vicksburg, Mississippi. Yup, the same Mississippi that Zig Ziglar grew up in saying that you can be anything you wanna be. (The Zig reference will make more sense in the next chapter.) For anyone who doesn't know, that ain't no regular American south. We're talking

Fannie Lou Hamer beaten by police while in jail Mississippi. We're talking Medgar Evers shot in his driveway a few years earlier for being a civil rights worker Mississippi. We're talking a Mississippi that inspired Nina Simone to write a song called "Mississippi Goddam". If you haven't heard that song, give it a listen. It will put everything that I'm about to tell you into perspective. I put a video of Nina Simone singing it over on the free download that comes with this book. Just go over to *thisiswhereitallends.com* and download your free download. It's still free. Cool? Cool.

Anyway, you get the idea. So, there was my mom, a teenager in that very same Mississippi and it was time for her to make her way into this world and start to figure out how to live. Part of that living meant that she needed to learn how to make her own money. Back then she said that the only job that she could get in her hometown of Vicksburg was cleaning houses. Segregation was the law of the land and in Mississippi the people in power were all for it. I can't even imagine what it was like being her in that situation.

She told me a story about how one time when she was walking home from school she needed to go to the bathroom. She saw a gas station on the horizon and thought, "Great! If I can just make it to the gas station, I can go to the bathroom." She then said that she walked into the gas station and asked where the bathroom was and the owner told her that she couldn't use it. It was for his white customers only. That happened to my mom. Not my great grandma or even my grandmother. My mom! Yeah… that stuff wasn't as long ago as they would like to have you think. Those limiting ideals and beliefs are a part of what has shaped us today and like I titled this book, This is where all that ends!

She said that she had to keep walking down the street and jump off into the woods to go to the bathroom. Yeah…As a sixteen or seventeen-year-old back then I don't know if I would have made it. However, when my mom was given lemons at any time in life, she always made lemonade. If the question "what can I learn from this" had a poster child, my mom was it.

So, she got a job cleaning houses and saved her money and eventually moved to Oregon with a job study program, but I digress. One of the things she took away from that whole situation was the thought that if those racist people she cleaned house for deserved a clean house, she DEFINITELY deserved a clean house. So, when she grew up and had kids of her own, she made sure that we understood that having a clean home was something that you did for yourself. You cleaned the house because you deserved a clean house. It was a sign of self-love. It was a sign of self-respect. So, as a kid we cleaned our house like it was our job every Saturday because every Saturday it actually was our job. *"Cleanliness is next to godliness,"* she would always say. The way that our house looked every Saturday evening, us and God could have been next-door neighbors. For real for real.

There was a cool benefit that I experienced from the whole thing aside from learning how to clean. One thing that I remember about being a kid in the Horne house was that I never lost anything. I never spent more than five minutes looking for something, because there was a place for everything, and everything was in its place. In Katie Horne's house if something didn't have a place, it belonged in file 13 (i.e. the trash) and my mom had no problem putting it there. As a matter of fact, if something of mine ever did come up missing, the trash was the first place I would check. My mom did not play! If you left stuff out, that meant that you didn't need it as far as she was concerned. I pulled a lot of things out of the trash when I was a kid, but eventually I learned to put things in the right place.

Later, when I moved into my own place, I decided that I was going to do things a little differently. Things could be a little more "lived in" in my place. You know how we do as young adults. We rush to find our "freedom" and that means we usually do all the things our parents told us NOT to do. We go out into the world, we get around all of our friends and their new "knowledgeable" ideas on life, #dontgetmestarted and we push back against all of those "old-fashioned rules" that our parents enforced when we were kids. Then about two months later (if we're lucky) we realize why our parents put those rules in place. I wasn't that lucky. My learning curve took years.

I was so disorganized it was ridiculous. I remember spending forty minutes looking for my keys one time. My lack of organization had me late to appointments, stressed out, and constantly looking for things. It had me basically living life in a chaotic mess. I wish that I could say that this was a once in a lifetime thing, but it happened to me a lot. All because I wanted to show my mom that I could do life without having everything all neat and organized.

During that illustrious time in my life, I ended up buying things that I already had. I did that a lot back then. Why? Because I couldn't find the first one of the thing that I was looking for. So, I would go out and buy another one because it was quicker than rummaging through my apartment. I had duplicates and triplets of things that I shouldn't have duplicates and triplicates of all because I wouldn't organize my house and throw needless crap away. I guess I showed her! #sarcasm

That is what a lot of us do, but we do it with our thoughts. As kids we are born with an understanding of who we are. We know that we are valuable. We come here with an inner knowing of who we are and who we're supposed to be. Then we run out into the world and we allow other people to give us limiting belief on top of limiting belief. We stockpile those little gems inside our minds like I did with all the duplicates of stuff that I had already bought. We end up with half-baked ideas about what is possible and what is impossible for us based on other people's opinions. We become an off course mental mess with a mind filled with piles of mental trash.

Look, if I were to look inside your mind right now, I bet that I would see all kinds of non-helpful thoughts hiding between the couch cushions of your mind. Stuff would be laying out all over your mental living room floor and that's not even the worst part. The worst part about all of this is that you have been hoarding these thoughts and holding on to them for years. You've even been defending them to anyone who came by and told you that you needed to clean them up.

You've been a trash beliefs hoarder. Those beliefs have been inside your head so long that now you claim them as your own. Maybe that trash belief was originally your friend's, maybe it was your cousin's, maybe it was a teacher's, maybe it was your mom's or your dad's. Who knows and who cares? All that matters is that until today you haven't thrown it away.

Right now, it's time to put those thoughts into your own mental file 13. It's time for your Katie Horne style mental Saturday morning gospel clean up.

So how do you to that? Let's cut the crap and get to work. Here's how we did it. Saturday mornings, we would all get a list of what we were supposed to do. We looked at our list, groaned if we got something that we didn't like, and then without any pushback we got to work. Once our jobs were done and checked off by mom or dad, we were free to do whatever we wanted. Well, not whatever we wanted, but we could go outside and play or just lounge around.

You and I are going to do the same thing. We are going to start your mental cleanup process with a list. Time to start cleaning and stop hoarding. This is your intervention.

☐ *Chore 1: Throw away some of your biggest beliefs about how life works.*

Your current way of thinking has produced the life that you are living right now. If you are wanting something different, you are going to have to change your way of thinking. For me, one of the major changes that I

60

had to do was to change the way that I looked at money. Your first thing might be something different. I used to think that money was the root of all evil. I used to think that money was scarce and hard to come by. Money made me afraid! That was my biggest belief about how life works. So that's the first thing I had to change.

When I was younger, I was afraid to look at my bank account. Real talk. I wouldn't check my bank account balance until I had a check to deposit. I did that so I wouldn't have to see how low it was. Plus, if it was low, I knew that it was about to go up because I was getting ready to put a check in there. Back then, I didn't know what to do so I would just hope and pray that my financial situation would work out.

That hoping and praying your situation will get better crap doesn't work. Faith without works is DEAD! I had to get to work and so do you. Right now, you need to find that one big fear belief that has been holding you back and challenge it. Work on conquering it and then move it out.

Holding on to my old way of thinking led to my car being repossessed, it led to my credit being ruined, and it led to me paying $40 dollars for a Wendy's frosty and cheeseburger.

Yup, you read that right. I once paid $40 dollars for a Wendy's frosty and cheeseburger. There I was on the heels of being a Broadway star and due to my old ways of thinking I was broke. I had made some bad business decisions based on bad information and emotions. Because of my bad decisions we were basically homeless. We moved in with my in-laws as we tried to figure out our next move.

On this particular day, Elizabeth's mom was making dinner for us because, as I said, we were living with them. My pride had me "tired" of eating their home cooked meals so I was going to do something about it. The idiot level was high with this one. What did ya boi do? I went to "treat" myself with a Wendy's cheeseburger and a mini frosty on my way home. Another "power grab" of idiotic proportions. That's what happens when your old-fashioned beliefs tell you things like, "You've been working hard. You deserve a break." Or in this case a "treat."

Your new mentality won't do that to you. Your new mentality will tell you something different. The new mentality tells you that you deserve a break when the job is done and not before. I knew that our account was beyond low, but I was sure that I had at least two dollars in there and we were getting paid the next day, so I went for it. That Wendy's burger treat was going to be mine! (Insert evil laugh here.)

Looking back on the whole thing, I have no idea how this broke ass kid thought that he deserved a "treat," but there I was in the Wendy's drive-through. I put in my order and pulled up to the window. As I handed the cashier my card, I held my breath. I was thinking to myself, "Please God, let this go through." Having your debit card declined for a two dollar and eight cent transaction would have been pretty embarrassing. I mean, it's a debit card, so if that gets declined that means that you are broke broke.

The cashier handed my card back and I celebrated with a little internal happy dance. I didn't have to be embarrassed AGAIN and I was going to have my "treat." There I was treating myself to a burger and a shake that I didn't even know if I could afford, but in my mind I had claimed a little power back. #dumb

I ate the burger and drank the chocolate shake as I drove to their house. When I got to my in-laws, I sat down for dinner. We did our small talk thing as we ate and then after dinner, I went upstairs to our room super full now. I mean, I had cheeseburger with extra pickles, a chocolate shake plus a complete dinner in my stomach so I was stuffed. I sat down and fired up the desktop to take a look at our bank account. I thought that I would check it and see how close we got to zero that month. We were getting paid tomorrow and it was after hours so in the morning I was going to wake up to a nice little deposit.

I typed in my password and my heart dropped through the floor. The account was overdrawn. There was a thirty-five-dollar overdraft fee staring me dead in the face. That two-dollar Wendy's transaction had cost me forty dollars! Well. thirty-seven dollars and eight cents to be exact.

That is what happens when you don't change major beliefs. You end up going through life struggling with the same issues over and over again because YOU don't change.

In my case it was the thought that "I deserve this" and "I deserve that." I didn't deserve anything. The world didn't owe me nothing. If I wanted to have more I was going to need to do more. I was going to have to change. I was going to have to throw away some of those old limiting beliefs that I had been holding onto. I was going to have to stop being a mental trash hoarder. If you want a better life you are going to have to work for it. You are going to have to earn it.

I had to change my thoughts and my mindset before any change could come to my life. You will have to do the same thing. Be willing to change your thoughts about life. Be willing to throw away head trash that isn't serving you. Be willing to do it and start to do it now!

So, chore one! Find that biggest baddest old fashioned limiting belief and get rid of it. You know what it is. It's time to look it in the face, give it a big hug and put it in the trash.

☐ *Chore 2: You are going to need to understand that life improvement is a solo journey.*

Most of the people that you know are not going to understand what you are doing. Now that you know that . . . the absolute WORST thing that you could do to yourself during this process of getting your mind right would be to share your journey with the people you know.

When I started out on my journey toward my greater self my greatest naysayers were people that I knew. Every person that I know who has done anything extraordinary struggled with what I call the "Et tu, brute?" syndrome and every time it was a surprise to them. Don't be one of those people.

You probably will be one of those people because it seems to be human nature to learn the hard way, but at least you won't be as surprised as we all were when your moment comes. Nobody told me that this was even a thing. That's why I am telling you now. We gotta level up. Each one teach one.

What's the "Et tu, Brute?" syndrome you ask? Well. . . .

In the play *The Tragedy of Julius Caesar*, Julius Caesar had just led Rome to a huge victory on the battlefield. The people of Rome were rejoicing and praising Julius' accomplishments. Yup, that's right. He was actually winning, and he was helping other people win. Sounds like a great thing, right? WRONG! Not according to his friends and those closest to him.

You see, Caesar's friends and family didn't like that he was getting all the attention. His friends, Brutus and Cassius, were super bothered by the whole Julius for emperor chanting thing despite him being "deserving" of the role. (Apparently, I used quotations a lot to signify my sarcasm. Who knew?)

Caesar's two "friends" got jealous because they didn't want him to win more than they were winning. Yup, that's how it goes down in these streets, but like the infomercial says, "But wait, there's more!"

During the ceremony that put these "friends" of Caesar's over the edge, Julius was offered the crown three times by the Roman people. Yup, the Roman people were so happy about all of the things he was doing for them that they offered to crown him their emperor three times. He didn't feel like he deserved it so he turned it down not once, not twice, but three times. He was all,

"Hey folks, thanks for all of the 'here's the crown be our emperor' stuff, but I just want to keep helping y'all out. I don't want to be your emperor or anything. Let's just keep doing what's best for everyone and leave it at that."

However, his homies only saw that he was getting all of the attention. They weren't about to have that happen. In their minds their friend Jay Cee was getting a little uppity, too big for his britches some might say, a little full of himself if you know what I mean. Instead of celebrating with him they start spreading rumors about him. They started talking about all of the reasons why he shouldn't be Rome's ruler. They even went as far as to talk about why he should be killed. These dudes were WILDIN'! Crabs in a bucket syndrome was on tilt!

So they were gossipin' gossipin' and murder plottin' and murder plottin' and Cesar catches wind that these rumors are being spread about him. He turns to his best friend Brutus for support. He was like, "Yo Brutus. I hear that a lot of these Roman Council dudes don't want me to be emperor. To be honest, I don't really want to be the emperor either, but the people kept saying that that was the best way for me to serve them so that's what I did.

Now I hear that some of these cats are not only lying on me, but they are also trying to kill me bro. Glad to know that at least you got my back."

Enter Brutus's side eye when Julius ain't looking.

Just like many people who start rising to the top Julius found out that those closest to him were the ones who wanted to sabotage him the most. He knew that Cassius was up to no good, but he and Brutus had been boys for a minute so he thought that Brutus would have his back. Well, like many people who fall into that "Et, tu Brute?" trap that I'm trying to keep you out of, he was wrong.

As a matter of fact, Brutus was the last person to stab him. Just before he died, Caesar looked up and saw Brutus coming. I'm sure that he was thinking, "Thank God. My homeboy is here. He's going to make sure I'm good and then wreck these fools." But that ain't what happened. Brutus stabbed him too. That's when he looks up at Brutus and said, "Et tu, Brute?" which basically translates to "You too, Brutus?"

It's wild out here in these streets my friend. Don't get caught slippin'. Keep this process private until you get to where you want to go. The best time to kill a dream (or a transformation in this case) is when it is in infant stage. Left a great video about that on the download too. Go get it. It's still free and it's still waiting for you over at thisiswhereitallends.com

Lastly, before you go walking around giving all your friends the side-eye, remember this.

☐ *Chore 2: It ain't personal and it ain't about YOU. It ain't about your feelings. You're just not that important.*

Look, people's opinions of you and your transformation have nothing to do with you. You're not that important. I mean, you are important to you, but in the scheme of things none of us are that important to other people. How long did you mourn Nipsey Hussle? How about 2Pac? How about Dr. Martin Luther King, Kobe, Maya Angelou, or Malcolm X? Do you still mourn for Michael Jackson? Do you still remember Marcus Garvey or W.E.B. Du Bois or Booker T. Washington? How long did your cousin's mourn your grandma or grandpa passing despite all they did for y'all? How long did people mourn Cesar Chavez or Medgar Evers? Do y'all even really know who they are? Well, they were very important and popular during their time and they did a lot of good for a lot of people. Despite all that, we kept on living our lives even after they were gone. If we're honest we very rarely think of any them throughout our daily life.

When you go, everyone will do the same thing. They will keep going on with life. We are not as important as we think. Learning this helped me keep other people's opinions in perspective. Don't make anything a personal matter ever. Because it absolutely isn't. Taking things personally is a move of the ego and even though I believe that the ego is super necessary it can have its downfalls. As long as you remember that ain't nobody really thinking about you you should do fine.

Look, people want you to stay the same because it's good for them. People don't like change and they don't like you showing them that they can do better in life. Most people are cool with the status quo. No shade intended. That's just the way it is.

Most people don't want to have to go through the pain that comes with change and growth. See the caterpillar to a butterfly thing that's coming up in the next section. Change is hard and 99.9% of the time it hurts a lot. It's uncomfortable. You gotta remember that your friends and family didn't sign up for the changes that you are looking to make. They especially didn't sign up for the discomfort that comes with it. You did that. You signed up for a better life. You signed up for more time with your family. You signed up for more money. You signed up for a life that is filled with significance.

This transformation is a YOU thing. It is not a we thing. Plus, seeing you change will challenge their caterpillar-ness and some people like being caterpillars. They might complain about their life 24/7, but deep down inside most people like being where they are. They will fight you if you say that, but it's true.

Most people don't want to become a butterfly. They want to stay a caterpillar and keep complaining about not being able to fly. #truestory Look, it is not your job to make them understand or to change them. Your job is to make YOU understand. Your job is to work on changing you! This is an inside job. Keep your thoughts, transformations, level ups, process and prayers to yourself.

The worst thing that you can do is show people your cocoon while you are in the gooey transformation to a

STEP 3 – STOP BEING AN HTH!

beautiful butterfly. That's when you are most vulnerable. If anything crushes you during the mushy cocoon stage you won't make it to the beautiful butterfly part. You will stay in the goo stage forever.

Look, true story, when I was a kid I learned about the caterpillar and how it goes through the change in the cocoon. I learned that during the caterpillar transformation it is the most vulnerable. I learned that during that time there are a million things happening that can go wrong. I learned that if it is knocked off the branch that it's on it will die. I learned that if it is crushed during that time it dies. So, do you know what Troy the kid did when he found a cocoon? He knocked it down and then crushed it. Sure enough, black goo came out. Sure enough it was not going to come back from that.

To be honest, at that time I did feel sad. I felt bad that I had just crushed a potential butterfly. I felt bad that I had just killed something. That is for a few minutes. Then I went back to eating my peanut butter and jelly sandwich. That's exactly what I'm talking about. Don't share your dreams with people when you are just getting started. Keep it to yourself, because just like little Troy they will

73

feel bad for a few moments after they crush your dream, but they too will go back to eating their peanut butter and jelly sandwich.

Right now, you need to focus on saving yourself. As the airline flight attendant says at the beginning of a flight, "Put on your own oxygen mask before assisting the person next to you." You can't save the world if you haven't first saved yourself. Right now, you are in save yourself mode.

Do that first and don't take anything personally. Emotional responses are a sucka move. Don't be a sucka! Keep your dream to yourself and keep it moving.

☐ *Chore 3: Butterflies see a lot more life than caterpillars, but they have to die first.*

You are going to have to let your old self die. You are going to have to let your old ideas die. You have to let them go if you want to be the you that you were born to be. When a caterpillar changes into a butterfly it has to die in the process. The caterpillar's body liquifies itself and digests itself with its own enzymes. It liquifies ITSELF!! That's CRAZY!

The caterpillar is on a super mission of growth and change and while it's on that mission it is the most vulnerable. I don't know about you but digesting your entire body doesn't sound easy, but for those of us who have seen a butterfly it is definitely worth it.

On the flip side, the caterpillar can choose to stay a caterpillar for its entire life. People choose to be caterpillars their whole life every day. They choose to never soar through the clouds. They choose to never float on the wind above the trees. Staying a caterpillar means no new and exciting places to see, no new heights to reach, no new limits of life to break. All of those places and experiences are unreachable for a caterpillar, but they are an everyday event for a butterfly. The question is, will you make the change or stay the same? Only you know the answer. Just know that not making a decision is making a decision. It took me a while to learn that too. Ya' welcome.

Last but not least . . .

☐ *Chore 4: Absorb what is useful and discard the rest.*

Don't hold on to anything that isn't serving you. ANYTHING! (See the caterpillar thing again.) In order to fly above the clouds, that caterpillar throws away everything that doesn't help him fly. I'm watching that Formula 1 series on Netflix right now and they are moving and removing things to shave off tenths of a second. That is how important getting rid of anything that is not helping them reach their goal is.

In race car driving there is a lot of effort put into making the car as light as possible. Seats are designed differently, interior pieces that don't help the driver win are removed. Everything that doesn't contribute to helping the car move as fast as it possibly can is thrown away in the pursuit of efficiency. In horse racing the smallest lightest jockeys are used to make sure that the horse can run as fast as possible. In every effort to reach the goal, all of the un-useful parts are taken off and thrown away. Keep what is useful and throw away the rest. File thirteen is your friend.

"Absorb what is useful, discard what is useless and add what is specifically your own." – Bruce Lee

In the beginning it will be hard.

When I first moved to Los Angeles, I drove a 1985 Nissan Sentra. It was a stick shift, had no air conditioning, and had a tendency to overheat. The overheating part wouldn't have been a problem in the winter, but I decided to drive out to L.A. in the summer, because apparently even back then I loved choosing the hard way.

So, there I was, all by myself driving down I-10 from Houston to Los Angeles in my small silver Nissan Sentra. I stopped at a casino during my trip and put some money in a slot machine or two.

I was doing it! I was making it happen. No mom or dad to fall back on. It was all up to me. That was one of the most exciting times in my life. I remember pulling over to the side of the road multiple times to wait for the car to cool down in the middle of the desert. It was literally one hundred degrees outside, but I loved every minute of it.

During one of those overheating sessions, I was in the middle of that one-hundred-mile stretch on I-10 where there are no services. If you have ever taken that drive from Texas to California, you know that stretch very well. Back then we didn't have cell phones, at least I didn't, so when you were away from a landline you were out of reach for real. I kind of miss those days if I'm being honest.

Anyways, there I was a kid without a cell phone, out in the middle of the desert, in a silver Nissan tin can as happy as hell. I knew that things could go sideways real quick. Despite all of that, ya' boi was out there driving across the desert toward his dream. I was on my caterpillar vibe, and I wasn't going to be denied. Besides, I had a lot of people to prove wrong. A lot of my friends and family had already told me that I would be back. They were predicting my failure before I even got started. Well, hold my beer.. I was going for my change, and I wasn't coming back without it!

The next day I was on schedule to be driving into Los Angeles. I was a bit nervous, but there was no turning back now. I was in Cali. I pulled into the city that night at about nine o'clock or so and a chill of excitement swept over me. I can still see the San Fernando Valley all lit up in my mind. As I came over the hill on the 405 it was very clear that I wasn't in Kansas anymore. It was exciting and scary all at the same time.

It was late, so I stopped at a payphone and called my cousin who I was supposed to be staying with. They had invited me to stay with them when I got to L.A. and I wanted to make sure that it was OK to come on over that late. I knew that they had a little one in the house, and I didn't want to wake her up. I told them that if it was better, I could stay in a hotel and check in with them in the morning. They said to drive on up to the house and they would let me in when I got there. They gave me some final tips and directions on how to get to their house and I was on my way. I had my Triptik from Triple A so between that and their added tips I was good to go. (Shout out to all of you if you remember Tripple A's TripTiks!)

The minute that I pulled up to their house I could feel that I wasn't welcome like they said I was. The tension in the air was pretty thick and I had no idea why. I mean over the phone they had been all "This is going to be great!" and "We can't wait to see you." I had called them months before and told them I was coming. I told them the plan including the date that I would be traveling, and I had asked them if it was still OK pretty much every week up until then. I had even called to touch base along the way. So when I got there and they basically met me at the door, pointed me to the couch, and went back to their bedroom, it seemed a little weird. Buuut I was there, and I wasn't turning around now.

Long story short, they kicked me out the second week that I was there. As I remember they told me that they were trying to adopt and that a twenty-year-old guy sleeping on the couch was not a good look to the social worker. No matter what it was, I was homeless for the first time and now I had even less money than I had before. I called my dad and he pointed me to a friend of his girlfriend's who lived in Calabasas at the time.

For those of you who don't know, Calabasas is about an hour out of town. My dream chasing trip was not going as planned, but as the saying goes, when life gives you lemons, make lemonade. That's exactly what I did. Without going too far into the whole story of how this led to me laying carpet in commercial buildings the following week and then to finally getting a job working for Disney as a singer, let me say this.

Without that struggle I wouldn't have been focused enough to find any job. Without that initial test I would not have been ready for life as a musician in the big city. Without the decision to keep going, no matter what, I wouldn't have met my wife, starred on Broadway, started a successful multi-six-figure business, signed a record deal, toured the world, or lived in Japan.

Without the struggle I wouldn't have been able to soar. I told you all of that to tell you this. When you do finally decide to go for it, God, the universe, or whatever you want to call it will say something like, "Oh Yeah? Let's See." And then throw everything and the kitchen sink at you.

When you see those roadblocks and trials coming, don't give up. Know that you are going in the right direction. Understand that they are just a test, and that the only way to pass that test is to keep going. Embrace the struggle. It will be hard in the beginning, but it's beautiful on the other side.

Learn what you need to learn from the situation and let go of all the rest. What I learned was that

☐ You have to be ready to pivot at a moment's notice.

☐ Never get comfortable.

☐ Physical labor is invigorating, but not for me. Ha!

☐ If I had to make it happen, I have the make it happen gene.

81

and a lot of other cool stuff. I also learned that nothing is personal so leave your emotions out of it. Assess the situation and keep it moving.

"If there is no struggle there is no progress."

– Frederick Douglass

Your Third Assignment

List 5 beliefs that have been keeping you stuck that you're going to get out of your head today!

5 self-defeating, limited beliefs that I am getting rid of today.

_____

_____

_____

_____

_____

5 amazing, limitless beliefs I'm going to replace them with

_____

_____

_____

_____

_____

3 limiting beliefs that are up next for elimination.

_____

_____

_____

_____

_____

_____

3 limitless beliefs that I'm going to replace them with.

_____

_____

_____

_____

_____

_____

84

CHAPTER 4

STEP 4 – THE MENTOR FACTOR

Everybody can't be your mentor. Read that again! You have to find a mentor who knows your story, understands your struggle, and can see your target through your eyes. Your mentor needs to have either seen it before from where you're coming from, or they need to have hit the target before from where you're coming from. You have to find a mentor who knows your story.

For me that meant someone who was an African American male. For you it may be someone of the same economic class, or gender, or whatever, but they have to know your story from an "I've lived it from your experience" perspective. There are little nuances in life that you can be guided through only by people who have lived it. Look, I have been mentored by a lot of people and I got a lot out of each and every one of them, BUT the strongest results came when I mixed their advice with the advice from someone who knew my story.

I'm not saying that all of your mentors need to know your story from your perspective, but I am saying that at least a couple of them do. I know, I know, a lot of people don't like to talk about this stuff. A lot of people like to jump to the we are all one and we are all humans, but love it or hate it that ain't what it is. My wife is having a very different life experience from mine. My kids are having a very different life experience than the one that I've had. Also, we ain't got time to beat around the bush. Having a mentor who knew my life experience changed the game for me! They knew all the unsaid things about my situation. I didn't have to explain or defend all of the unsaid things that come with going after my dreams as an African American male. I didn't have to teach them. They already knew the context personally and that was huge.

Have you ever tried to take a test without taking the class? That's what mentoring without knowing your life experience personally is like. Anyone can read all the textbooks about boxing, but everything changes once you get hit.

> *"Everyone has a plan until they get punched in the mouth." – Mike Tyson*

Until you've had a class of "Life Experience 101" you can't understand the test and you definitely can't tutor or mentor someone for it. Funny not so funny story...

When my wife Elizabeth was pregnant with our first child, she had really bad morning sickness. She had to be hospitalized overnight. She had to have IVs and all of that stuff, but you couldn't have told "Pregnancy Expert Troy" that back then. To the "pregnancy expert," morning sickness was something that you could control with your mind. I mean, I had read all the self-help books out there and listened to all of the audio programs about how life is experienced as a result of your state and all of that other stuff is crap. You know, *Think and Grow Rich*, Tony Robbins and all of that stuff. "Thoughts are things" and "change your state change your life" all of that crap. There is some truth to that stuff, it's just not an absolute truth and a lot of times it is presented as an absolute truth. I just "knew" that the mind was super powerful and that if she didn't want to be sick, she could change everything with her mind.

There I was, twenty-nine-year-old Troy with all the advice in the world on pregnancy. There I was, a man who would never be pregnant, telling my pregnant wife how morning sickness was just a mental game and that if she didn't want to be sick all she had to do was to tell herself that she wasn't sick. She just needed to "pick herself up by her mental bootstraps" and tell her body that she wasn't doing nausea today.

All of this was said with a strong sense of righteousness, indignity, and confidence. Oh, and arrogant stupidity, did I mention arrogant stupidity?

How the hell would I know what morning sickness was like? Up until that moment I hadn't even been around someone 24/7 who was pregnant. Yet, I had all the answers on pregnancy and childbirth because I had read a book or two.

That's what having a mentor who doesn't know your story is like. They will have all the answers and most of the time it will be for the wrong questions. I have had mentors who didn't know my story who were very indignant about why my attempts were failing without knowing anything about a big part of my journey. They had no idea what my life was like and would never know, but they thought they did.

If there has been one thing that has been made clear recently, it's that there can be very different life experiences in this world even if you live in the same place. The fact that your journey has a lot of different unknown, unspoken factors is something that you must consider when choosing a mentor and yes, you choose your mentor.

I want you to think about something that I only came to understand as I got older. Napoleon Hill wrote in his book *Think and Grow Rich*:

"Whatever the mind of man can conceive and believe he can achieve." - American Author Napoleon Hill, 1937

I ain't gotta tell you that ANY woman or person of color might have seen things a little differently in 1937 America. Now, before you go all "Wait a minute. I thought that you said that *Think and Grow Rich* changed your life." Let me tell you that it did, but the point that I'm making by telling you all of this was that Mr. Hill didn't have the whole story. That's probably why his book hadn't made it into our family library when I was a kid.

During the beginning of my journey only a few of my virtual mentors knew my story. Only a few of my in-person mentors knew my story, but those few who did made a huge difference.

I love me some Zig Ziglar, but Zig was a kid in the 30s Mississippi, and an adult in 1950s South Carolina. He didn't have the same experience that my grandparents and my parents had back then. My mom grew up in Mississippi in the 50s. Her and Zig were probably not friends and probably couldn't have been friends if we're keeping it one hunnit. So, although the information that he gave me was super powerful, there are some major things about reaching my goal that Zig couldn't help me with.

Now before you go all Madame CJ Walker on me, let me clarify that I am not saying that you couldn't be successful in 1937, I'm just saying that you probably couldn't have been president of the United States. There were some limitations that thinking alone wouldn't have solved despite what Mr. Hill would tell you.

Earl Nightingale, Grant Cardone, Tony Robbins, Brendon Burchard, Tim Ferriss, and countless other entrepreneurs are all amazing dudes, but there are some pretty important parts to being successful as an entrepreneur that I am going to have to navigate that they can't help me with. Again, no knock on them, it's just what it is. There are some pretty big things that will show up in my life journey that are going to sound like make-believe to them. There are a lot of situations where their advice is going to sound like I did when I was telling my wife that morning sickness was a figment of her imagination.

Now does that mean they can't give me great information and great tips on how to take my life to the next level? No! More importantly is this a valid excuse as to why I "can't" equal or surpass their success and influence? No! (Again, see Madam CJ Walker) In fact, all of them have given me great guidance and advice along the way. HOWEVER, they can't be my only source of information.

For me, and this is just for me, my mentor pool MUST have some Dame Dash, some JAY-Z, some Oprah Winfrey, some Barack and Michelle Obama, and some Byron Allen.

I need some Earn Your Leisure, some Robert Smith, I need some Wall Street Trapper, I need some Les Brown, I need some Eric Thomas, I need some Marcus Barney, I need some Jay Morrison, I need some Master P. They not only know the success part, but they know my whole story.

Are you picking up what I'm putting down? Make sure that you find those mentors who know your story and add them to your mentor pool. It is an absolute must!

Like I said before, it's easy to tell somebody what to do when you ain't never been in their situation. But, if you do it from a purely academic understanding of the situation, nine times out of ten you are going to be confidently proclaiming the wrong advice just like I did to Elizabeth.

Yeah, I have no idea how I'm still married, by the way.

In the beginning, while you are finding that main mentor, you can still have mentors who don't know your story. They can still guide you and direct you in the early stages, but they can't be your only go-to for mentorship. Don't walk, RUN to find a mentor who knows your life experience. Just keeping it real.

I know that I've said it a lot in this chapter, but that's how important it is. OK, one last time and then I'm going to let it go.

> *"If they don't understand the nuances that are your life experiences, they can't be your main guide or mentor. If they don't know where you've been, they can't lead you all the way to where you want to go." - Troy Horne*

Now after all that, I have to say this.

There are a few exceptions, because if there is anything that life will teach you, it's that there are absolutely zero absolutes. There is nothing that is always true. Those exceptions are if they have mentees with your same experience who have been successful at what you want to do. I mean there are business coaches, sports coaches, and parents who have coached their kids, students, or clients on to successes that they themselves have never reached. If there is a track record, there is a difference. But that being said, I bet if you asked those success stories, they will tell you that what I said did play a factor in their success as well. Be sure to ask. Your success is on the line.

In closing, let me share with you what Denzel Washington said when he was asked why he thought that the movie *Fences* needed to have an African American director. He said, and I quote . . .

"Steven Spielberg could direct Goodfellas. Martin Scorsese probably could have done a good job with Schindler's List. But there are cultural differences. I know, you know, we all know what it is when a hot comb hits your head on a Sunday morning, what it smells like. That's a cultural difference." – Denzel Washington

And that, my friend, is what you should consider when putting together your mentor pool. We're talking about your life. It's not something that a lot of people like to talk about. It's not something that feels rosey and nice. It doesn't fit into the narrative that says that everyone is the same and has the same experiences. But if we're being honest, that way of thinking, though it may feel good, is not the truth.

There is a difference in life experiences. There is a difference in the way that different people have to walk this planet, and you can't understand it just by reading about it. Make sure that your mentor isn't just reading about it.

Make sure that you have the right director/mentor in place. It's important to have the right people in the right roles. Don't be so eager to fill the mentor role that you hire Quentin Tarantino to direct *Do The Right Thing*, all right? The video of Mr. Washington saying it does a lot better service to the quote than me writing it.

You can watch him saying it much better than me over on the free download. Just go to <u>thisiswhereitallends.com</u> and download your free bonus guide.

I think I have driven it home. Let's move on to the next step of your journey. But before we do that, let's do your homework assignment for this chapter.

Your Fourth Assignment

List 3 mentors, virtual or otherwise, that you are going to add to your mentor team.

_____

_____

_____

_____

_____

_____

List 3 things about them that qualify each of them to be your mentor. (Yes, you choose who has the privilege of mentoring you and YES, it is a privilege.)

Mentor 1 Qualification

_____

_____

_____

_____

_____

_____

Mentor 2 Qualification

_____

_____

_____

_____

_____

_____

Mentor 3 Qualification

_____

_____

_____

_____

_____

_____

CHAPTER 5

STEP 5 – STOP THE FLOW

As an entertainer it hurts my heart to say this, but here it goes: Your entertainment IS your subconscious programming and 99.9% of it is absolute TRASH! That is if you want to be successful in life. The Matrix is real my friend and you are living in it. I bet that if you took a look around your life right now you would see that in some way, shape or form, your life is reflecting the music that you listen to, the movies or television that you watch, and the entertainment that you run to after a hard day at work.

I have had the pleasure of knowing multiple millionaires in my life. Do you know what was common among all of them? None of them knew what the hottest show was on Netflix. None of them knew the lyrics to the top 10 songs on Billboard, and none of them spent their days consuming anything that could negatively program their subconscious mind.

Right now, you may be addicted to the drug called pop culture. It is my job to tell you that if you are addicted to that drug you are filling your subconscious mind with self-defeating messages and programming. There I said it. From this moment on you can't say that nobody told you.

They Call TV Shows "Programming" For A Reason

You have to detox yourself from the media addiction in order to get back to your original self. When you were a kid you had no limitations. You had no negative self-talk. You had the mindset of a world changer. You had the mental fortitude of a winner at the game of life.

You need to get that person back. In order to get them back you are going to have to turn off the flow of other people's programming. There is no other way around it. You have been letting someone else tell you what your goals should be. You have been letting someone who doesn't know you from Adam tell you what your life should look like. That's crazy when you think about it.

I remember becoming aware of this when I lived in Japan for a year. Gradually my ideas on life changed. What was acceptable changed. What was expected changed. My ideas changed because my perspective and understanding changed. Do you know what also changed? My entertainment. Japanese television places importance on different things. It isn't American programming. There are different values. I'm telling you, the shows that you are watching are that powerful. You are going to have to change your "programming" if you are going to change your life.

I used to listen to hip-hop and R&B a lot. Later on in college I listened to rock music. I had to know what was hot and what was not. I was a professional musician. It was a part of my craft. However, as I got older, I stopped. As soon as I realized that those lyrics and those words were shaping my life, I traded them in for books on tape. As soon as I got my car back from the repo man I put that *Think and Grow Rich* audio book in the car and played it over and over again on repeat. To this day I still don't listen to music in my car. Well, there is one exception. I do listen to jazz, but aside from that it's audiobooks.

A long time ago, a friend of mine gave me an MP3 with this guru guy on it. The meditation was supposed to be one that helped me make a shift from my limiting beliefs to unlimited beliefs. I was willing to give it a shot because, despite having achieved the goal of working as a musician full time, I wasn't seeing my family nearly enough. I had gained my career and lost my time. For the record, I basically saw my family for about two hours a day. We got up in the morning and did the morning rush and then on the way home I would pick up some dinner or come home to cook. Then I would head to bed around 8:30 to do it again the next day.

There I was about a month into this process of listening to this mantra thing as I drove to work (or should I say scooted to work for those of you who have experienced Los Angeles rush hour traffic). Then suddenly it happened—I had another Viola Davis breakdown moment. (Apparently, I'm a crier.) This time it was because I was stressed out. I had just told the casting office for the Broadway show RENT that I wasn't going to do the show the day before because going on the road with the tour would have meant even less time with my family. On top of that, on this particular day I had just dropped my kid off at daycare and he was crying about being left there for the day. I guess I was crying because I didn't want to have to leave him there. For those parents who know the struggle, it's real!

Let me rewind because I haven't told you the RENT story yet.

The Story About How I Ended Up In RENT on Broadway!

Earlier that month I had a day off from my job at Disneyland. During that day off I went to an audition for the Broadway show RENT. This was after the car repo event, and after I had been listening to nothing but self-help for a while. I was all in on making the mental shift and I had heard that listening to music while you were in the car was a waste of subconscious brain power. Basically, Zig Ziglar had said on one of those tapes—or maybe it was Brian Tracy—either way, one of them had said that you should turn your car into an automotive university. It was Brian Tracy… Anywhoo.

I had done that. My car became self-help university. One of the most amazing things that happened was that 1. I became a lot happier and 2. I was having different internal conversations with myself during the day.

On this day off I went to Barnes and Noble and picked up the Back Stage West. It was still Backstage West back then and that was where you learned about all of the new entertainment industry jobs that were out there. I flipped it open and that's when I saw that audition for RENT. I checked the date of the audition, and it was that very same day. As a matter of fact, the audition had already started and was going to be ending in a couple of hours.

I almost put down the paper, but that's when that quiet voice that was usually drowned out by the whatever morning show or top new rap song beat that would have been usually bouncing around my head, spoke to me and said, "If you go to this audition, you will get this job." It was as loud and as confident as any voice that I had ever heard in real life. So, do you know what I did? Ya boi called his wife and asked her if she would be willing to move to New York.

Yeah... it was like that. There I was, her dreamer husband on the phone talking about moving to New York for a Broadway show that I hadn't even auditioned for yet. I just knew that I was going to get this show if I went to the audition. The quiet voice had told me so and I was all in. I had to make sure that she took this one seriously, because according to that quiet voice, this train was about to leave the station. After a short conversation, she said that she would be happy to move if I were to get the part, and the die was cast. I bought the trade paper because back then our phones didn't have cameras and I needed the address. Went out to my car and headed off to the audition.

When I got to the audition, two people were in the waiting room. The monitor, or the person who signs people in for you non auditioning folks, was reading a paper and other than that it was pretty empty. I walked right up to the desk and signed in. The monitor asked me if I would be ready to go in about fifteen minutes and I said I would. For those of you who are not familiar with the Los Angeles audition process, that is NOT how this stuff typically goes. Usually, you sign in and go get a snack or something because your wait is about an hour or so, especially for a Broadway Show. I couldn't believe that I was basically signing up and walking into an audition!

I played it cool and went to my car to warm up. I sang through my usual vocal exercises and then came back into the audition waiting room. As soon as I got back, she said, "We're ready for you now!" and I walked right in. It was CRAZY!

Immediately after my first song they asked me to sing another one. I was so green! I had two songs and that was literally it. So, I sang my second song and then they asked me to stick around for the dance part. My heart nearly exploded. I'm not a dancer to say the least and I knew it. I mean, I can dance in the club, but that on stage choreography stuff isn't my strong suit. We did the dance stuff and I definitely wasn't great. Then after the dance part of the audition they said the words that every actor dreads to hear, "Thank you! We'll be making calls later on this week." Those words usually mean, "You ain't it. Nice try though chief."

This time, however, it actually meant we'll be making calls later on this week. A couple of days later my phone rang. On my phone was this New York number. I typically didn't answer calls back then because usually unknown numbers were from bill collectors, and I was still working out the bill collector part of my life. Anyway, I looked at it for a while and then that same voice told me to answer the phone, so I did. "Hello." I answered. For those bill dodger folks out there, you know that you never say, "Hello this is Troy" or anything like that because you don't want them to know they got the right person. Man, I am so glad that those days are behind me.

Anyway, on the other end of the phone was the casting director for the show. "May I speak to Troy Horne please," she said, totally unaware of the situation that was happening on the other end of the call. "May I ask who's calling?" I answered.

"It's Brenda from Telsey." My heart jumped. Telsey was the casting company for the Broadway show RENT. They were actually calling me back! During the call, she offered me a spot on the Broadway tour. She went over all the specifics, the pay and all that stuff, and my jaw dropped. It was going to be a lot more than what I had been making at my current job. The problem was that it was a tour. That meant that I was going to be on the road. That also meant that I was going to have even less time with my family.

It hurt to say no, but I knew that it would hurt even more to see my family even less. We hung up and I went through all of the self-doubt that we all go through when it seems like our dreams have been dashed:

"You failed again. Dude you're such a weirdo."

"Want to move to New York when I get this role for a show that I haven't even auditioned for? What a moron. How are you gonna explain this one dumbass?"

"You should have taken it. Who turns down an opportunity to make more money?"

Those are just a few of the gems that were on blast in my mind. I drove to Christmas Caroling rehearsal later that day because I had a musical side hustle to go with my musical main hustle. The great thing about the Christmas Caroling was that my wife and I were working this job together. Win win! I pulled up to the rehearsal and told her about what had just happened. She consoled me because she's a nurturer and we went inside to caroling practice.

That's when I went and shared it with other people. (See the keep your dreams to yourself section of this book coming up later and the etu brute section that you just read.) Some were just blown away that I would turn down a job that made more money. Others told me that I had blown my chance to be in the show. According to them, the tour was the only way to get on the Broadway show. Some of them had even auditioned before and hadn't gotten a call back. The fact that I had gotten a call back and then got offered the job and then turned it down meant that I wasn't going to hear from them ever again, according to some of my friends. According to them I had blown my chance. My wife consoled me and said something like, "That's OK sweetie. We're fine. Something else will come along."

Which brings us to about two weeks later. New morning, same story. I had just dropped off my crying kid again and I was down in the dumps because I had been beating myself up the entire week.

"I want my manifestation now!" chanted the voice of the mp3 guru over my classic ipod. I had one of those deals with the spin wheel on it. Remember those? "I want my manifestations now!" I screamed in the car as I drove down the 1-10 freeway. Then, just like before, it happened again. A New York number appeared on my caller ID. I quickly turned down the strange shanti shanti music and answered the phone.

It was Brenda from Telsey again. A spot had opened up on Broadway and she wanted to see if I would be open to coming in to audition for it. I couldn't believe it. I said yes of course and then hung up the phone and called Elizabeth. I had been invited to audition for producers for the Broadway show! I couldn't believe it. We still had no money, but we borrowed from Peter to pay Paul and made the audition happen.

I got on a plane to New York that weekend. Took a gypsy cab to the audition, stayed in one of the nastiest hotels that I had ever stayed in in my life. To put it in perspective the check in desk was behind plexiglass and this was way before the pandemic made it cool. The room was so gross that I slept in my clothes that night. I thought that I had done OK in the audition, but again they said thank you and I left the audition room without a job.

I called Elizabeth when I got back to the hotel and we talked about the whole thing. Of course, my mind went straight to how are we were going to make up for the money that we just spent on flights and the hotel. Anyway, when I got back to Los Angeles I let it all go and got back to the daily grind.

Later on that week the phone rang again and on the other end this time was Brenda with an offer to do the Broadway show.

That is the power of your mind and your intention, but you have to turn off all of those mental distractions in order for it to do what it was made to do. Turn your car into a university on wheels. Turn your car into a manifestation mobile. Turn off all of the stuff that they program you with for free and choose to program yourself with the messages and thoughts that you need to become the person you were made to be. Turn off the flow of self-defeating programming and a dash of limiting beliefs and your life will change.

Stop letting people who don't know you dictate the programming that happens in your own mind. Program yourself.

The Day Job And The Oscar Winner

(My Story Part 1)

I used to work at this survey place with Oscar winner Octavia Spencer back in the day. (More on that later in the book too.) I was the host for some of those focus group sessions where producers ask random people for their opinions on how a television show or movie should go.

They are literally writing shows based on random people's opinions. The way that it worked back then was that we would call people and invite them to be a part of this focus group for one hundred to two hundred dollars. Then the people who accepted the offer would come to the consumer testing place and give their opinion on the product, food, or show that was the subject of the evening. These people would then talk amongst themselves and give the product a thumbs up or a thumbs down.

So basically, a random sampling of people off the street are the ones that you are letting program you and your family. That's right random people who you don't know are telling you and your family what success looks like, what love looks like, what happiness looks like. Isn't that crazy?! Don't let random people who know nothing about your life program you.

OK, Troy. So what do I listen to? What do I watch? Where do I start? I got you. I put some of the books that started me off over on the download. Did I mention that the free download is still FREE? Yup! Still free. Go to thisiswhereitallends.com and get your free copy of the download. Oh, and make sure that you get the audio versions of those books and play them in your car.

Stop letting some random people program your life. Program your own damn life. Listen to books and audio programs that will make your life better. They are game changers! Start programming yourself. Your dream life is waiting for you! As Les Brown says as you go through life you are going to fall into one of two categories someone who works on their own dream or someone who works on someone else's dream. You decide.

Your Fifth Assignment

List 5 books, podcasts, or YouTube channels that you are going to subscribe to and listen to going forward. You can even list the ones on the download to start, but definitely list five and change the flow.

_____

_____

_____

_____

_____

_____

CHAPTER 6

STEP 6 – THE MANIFESTATION CREATION GUIDE

In the past, the words "Anything Is Possible" only really applied to certain people. There were gatekeepers, and gatekeepers for those gatekeepers. Physical barriers to your success literally stood in your way. They were not imagined. They were not in your head. They were very real. That was then and this is now!

Today there are literally no barriers between you and any goal that you wish to achieve. Now obviously if your goal is to play in the NFL and you are forty-seven and have never played a lick of football in your life, then you're probably not going to play in the NFL. I will never say that anything is impossible, but as far as physical goals like becoming heavyweight champion of the world after your fiftieth birthday goes: that might be a little bit out of reach. Of course, you have George Foreman who became heavyweight champion at forty so scrap everything that I just said, but you get the idea.

Basically, the point I'm trying to make is that today there are no gatekeepers. Anyone can go online and broadcast their message to the world. Today everyone has an audience. Anyone can reach anyone at any time. The only person standing in your way is you and your old-fashioned ideas about how things work. Or should I say someone else's old-fashioned ideas that YOU are still holding on to.

For instance, take my story of becoming a Broadway star. A lot of people think that my story is a once in a lifetime story that could never happen to them. Some of them were in the room that day when I shared my news about turning down the Broadway tour. They thought that it was a rare chance thing that would only come around once in a lifetime, but they were wrong. The same impossible goal-reaching powers are inside you too. You just got to know how to bring them out. In this chapter I am going to show you how to tap into your superhuman manifestation powers. I'm going to show you how to manifest.

There are two things that I did that made this happen and they are so simple to do, but most people never do them. The first of those things is your power to speak whatever you want into existence. This is not a new power. In fact, it's very old. The problem with most people is that they have been speaking the things that they don't want to happen into existence. Time to start speaking the things that you DO want to happen into existence.

Step 1: Speak It Into Existence

In the bible it says that God spoke the world into existence. It didn't say that God worked hard and grinded for years on end. It says that he spoke it and it was done. Now I'm not trying to make this into a religious sermon or anything. I'm just using that story as a reference. The power of your words is life changing. You can literally speak your world into existence. I know it's true because I did it. I still do it every day.

Speaking your world into existence isn't special or specific to just me. Lavar Ball did it with his sons. He said that all three of his sons would be in the NBA. Later he then said that Gelo wouldn't make it to the NBA and so far he has been right. Now could Gelo have created a different reality for himself? Of course, we all have the power to create our reality through our words, however, I don't think that Gelo understands the power as well as his father Lavar does. The question isn't will speaking your existence into reality work for you. The question is, will you do it? Here's the catch. Speaking your world into existence works all of the time.

When you say things that you don't want to happen in your life you are creating them as well. You are actually speaking the things that you don't want to happen into existence. Words are like the honey badger. They don't care. You say it, they make it happen. You're a real-life Aladdin and your words are your invisible genie!

You don't have to speak anything into existence that you don't want to be a part of your reality. Now before you go any further, I want to be clear that I am not saying to ignore things that go wrong in your life and pretend they're not there. The whole "Only Positive Vibes" movement is a crock of crap in my opinion and to be honest it's quite detrimental to the people using it; plus, super annoying!

Just because you don't want to look at the train wreck doesn't mean that the train wreck doesn't exist. It still exists, my ostrich friend. Actually, acknowledging that things aren't going well is a big step in becoming a capable adult.

All that I am saying is that you don't have to continue to confirm and affirm situations that you don't want. For instance, let's start with a pretty popular negative manifestation: "I can't afford it." That is an instance where you are probably speaking something into existence that you don't want to be your reality. Unless, of course, you're a person who doesn't want to be able to afford things. Instead, you can say, "How can I afford it?" or "I need to look into how I can make that happen," or you can be as straightforward as saying, "I really don't want it that bad." All those things are things you can say that don't put limits on your unlimited subconscious mind or your unlimited, life-creating abilities. It really is a game of you vs. you.

Also, just for the record, you need to be careful about doing this in public in the beginning. Some of the closest people to you will sabotage your goals and dreams if you say your positive life creating manifestations out loud. A lot of the people you know will plant seeds of doubt when you start to create your future using the power of your words. So only do it when you're alone or do it inside of your head in the beginning. Nobody needs to be a part of this process. Remember the infant stage video on the download? Yeah…do that. Yup, the download is still free and still available over at thisiswhereitallends.com.

If people try to sabotage you, they aren't doing it to be spiteful. Well, most of them aren't. Most of the time they are doing it from a place of love, if you can believe that.

They see your goals as something that seems impossible to them, and they don't want you to be disappointed. The problem is that they don't know what you know now. They don't know that you are working on your unlimited creation powers and that even though failure is inevitable along your path, they don't know you're cool with failing in order to get to your goal. They don't know that you know that failure is a part of the process. They don't know that you know that you're going to have to fall down seven times. Oh, but when you get up that eighth time you are going to be ready for the world. They just don't know what you know.

So as eager as you are to share your newly found knowledge with other people—as much as you want them to know about the power of speaking your world into existence—don't share this part of your journey with people yet. Keep it to yourself for now. Allow yourself to learn and validate this newly discovered superpower before you share with others. Remember what they did to Lavar? Remember how they called him crazy and how they told him that he can't just speak things into existence. Remember how quiet they got when his son Lonzo got drafted? Yeah... Wait until you get to expert level before you share your new found superpower. Let them see the results of your work. As the saying goes, "Don't announce your moves. Confirm your arrivals."

Stage one: Speak the reality you want to see into existence. Every day, every hour, every minute. Speak the life you want into existence.

Step 2: Write It Into Existence!

Your second superpower is writing down your goals every day. Over on the download I have a picture of what writing down my goals did for me. I don't like sharing my goals, but since we are fam like that, I will share one of them. Before I wrote this goal down I had a dream of helping over 1000 people in one month. That would mean that I would need to serve about 33 people a day. Normally I would say that you should 10x your goal like I did in this book, but I didn't have the guts back then so I 5x'ed my goal and said that I needed to serve 150 people a day. That would mean a revenue of about 1k a day in sales for that particular business.

So I wrote it down in the simplest form possible. Long story short, I hit my goal and blew past it as you're gonna see on the download. It happens all the time now that I know how this superpower works. Did you know that we are 42% more likely to achieve our goals if we just write them down? Writing your goals down every day is just like multiplying that possibility by a million.

The problem is that it's so simple it's hard. Most people lack the tiny amount of discipline it takes to write

121

down your goals every day. For the record, I write down my goals twice a day. I write them down in the morning when I wake up and at night when I go to sleep. I ain't taking no chances and you shouldn't either. Write down your goals!

Writing down my goals has a proven track record for me and my life, so I double down. The beautiful thing about writing down your goals is that it ends the negative talk. Writing down your goals ends the limited life beliefs that you have been experiencing. Writing down your goals catapults you into abundance. Writing down your goals is like affirmations for your subconscious mind. You're sending your instructions straight to the brain!

Now when you first write down your goals you are going to be in your head. At least that was the story for me. I was my own doubting Thomas for a long time. That's why I tell you to keep it to yourself in the beginning. You gotta win the battle with your own mind first. You are going to hear all the reasons why you are wasting your time. You are going to hear all those self-defeating reasons about how you aren't worthy of reaching your goal. You are going to hear all the voices of the past telling you all the reasons why you aren't good enough, talented enough, whatever enough. When you hear those voices, keep writing.

When you keep writing it down your other voice starts to chime in. It's going to say things like, "Why not you?" Your quiet voice is going to follow your lead and start telling the other voice things like, "Hey, if that other guy can do it why can't you do it? He ain't that special." You will actually make a shift from telling yourself all of the reasons why you can't reach your goals to being borderline offended that anyone (including yourself) who would say that you can't reach your goals. That confident five-year-old will be back! That's the power of the second step. It's literally magic.

Step two: Write down your goals twice a day until they manifest. It may take a year. It may take two. Keep writing.

Step 3: Ask And Your Subconscious Mind Will Do The Rest

The third step includes you asking the question: "OK, how can I do this?" You will shift from "I can't do this" to "why can't I do, be, or have that?" When you start asking yourself, "How do I do this?" This is where the magic starts to happen.

When you start asking yourself how can I reach my goal, opportunities that you didn't see before will start to appear. The *aha* moments start inside the stage of writing your goals down if you keep writing. That's the key: IF you keep writing.

A lot of people never make it through this stage. Most people write down their goals down once or twice and then forget about it. They say things like, "Ahh, that writing down your goals thing doesn't work." What they don't realize is that the plan will work if you work it, but you gotta work it.

Zig Ziglar tells a great story about water and wells. I put a link to it over on the download. The long and short of it is that you have to prime the pump of your manifestation powers. You have to put something in before you get something out. You are going to have to work for your dreams and it's going to take some time. He tells it better than I do, so get the download. It will all make sense.

> **Step three: When you write down your goals you will start to ask, "How can I do this?" and your subconscious mind will come back with the right answer.**

The Works

After you get through the first three steps you will reach step four. Step four is when it works. In step four you reach your goal. In step four you end up looking in the mirror and saying, "Damn! I can't believe that I pulled that off!" It's an amazing part of the journey. Live in it and love it because if you are like the rest of us, you will think that it was just a fluke in about a month. Enter the imposter syndrome! Yeah…that subconscious mind of yours is something else.

However, we all struggle with imposter syndrome. We all struggle with thinking that our success was just a fluke. So do you know what we do? We keep writing. We write down our next goals in spite of the doubt that will inevitably creep in. Feel the fear and do it anyway. Write down your goals and watch the magic happen. It's pretty awesome!

For many of us the imposter syndrome will never go away. Many of us will always feel like the other shoe could drop at any moment. Writing down your goals helps to combat that fear and doubt. As they say, the better you do the better you do.

Step four: Keep writing down your goals no matter what you do! Thank me later.

The How

Now, before you overcomplicate this stuff, let me share with you how I do this. I want to share the how with you because I struggled with the overthinking and analysis paralysis at the beginning too. Let my lessons learned through the pain of failure help you skip those steps. Let's move the ball forward.

How to speak your world into existence.

The first step is to keep it simple. A lot of people like to say things like, "This year I'll have more money than I've ever had before, I'll find the love of my life, and I'll move to this amazing city and live happily ever after." Ya' doing too much.

I know that some of you are going to have to learn the hard way, but here is what I did. I focused on one goal at a time. I followed the Muhammad Ali way of speaking things into existence. Do you remember what he said?

In 1964 before fighting Sonny Liston for the heavyweight title, Ali is quoted as saying, "I am the greatest!" That was it. I am the greatest!

When I used the speaking your life into existence superpower, I told my wife that I was going to get this job if I went into the audition. See how simple that is. I think that we get concerned we're going to miss something if we keep it that simple. We treat our subconscious mind like a five-star restaurant when it's really more like a buffet. We can still treat our subconscious mind like a five-star restaurant a little later in the process, but even at a five-star restaurant you can only order one entree at a time.

Keep that in mind when you are using your "speak your world into existence" superpower. Speak one thing into existence at a time. You will still be able to fill your plate with all of the goals and dreams that you want, you

127

just need to make sure to focus on one thing before you move to the next.

"My sons will play in the NBA." – LaVar Ball

"I'm the greatest of all time." – Muhammad Ali

"If I go to this audition, I'm getting this job." – Troy Horne

There are more, but you get the idea. Keep it simple.

How to write your world into existence.

The same thing goes for writing down your goals. Keep it simple. If you have the download, you can see what I mean, but for those of you still thinking about getting it, here is an example of what I mean. Simply write down the first goal. The famous motivational speaker Marie Forleo wrote down . . .

"I am a number one New York Times Best Seller."

She wrote that for her book *Everything Is Figureoutable*, she wrote those very words 15 times a day. Guess what? She is now a number one New York Times Best Seller.

When I set my goals, I made sure to keep my goals under 15 words. Do that! Keep it simple. Write down your goals in under 15 words. If you have to write more than 15 words you are doing too much partner. Don't do too much. Focus on one goal at a time. The buffet line of goals and dreams ain't going nowhere.

Keep it simple and check them all off as you go along. Video of Marie talking about how she did it over on the download too. Still free at thisiswhereitallends.com

Your Sixth Assignment

List 3 goals that you are going to achieve. The first goal is The Big Goal. The HUGE GOAL.

First Goal. Write in detail. (Goal in detail, 50 words or less, and the date you will reach it.)

_____

_____

_____

_____

_____

Write down a simple version of your big goal in 15 words or less.

_____

_____

_____

_____

_____

Go somewhere by yourself and read your goal out loud!

CHAPTER 7

STEP 7 – NO SUMMER SCHOOL

Speaking of everything being "figureoutable," the next step is key for the rest of your life. Now that you are writing things down and speaking your reality into existence. Now that you are clearing out all of those old limiting beliefs and taking responsibility for everything. There is one more thing to add to your repertoire. You have to commit to filling all of that newly freed up subconscious space with more of what you want.

Your subconscious mind is a juggernaut and, if we're being real, you can never fill it up. Your subconscious mind helps you breathe, blink your eyes, and keep your heart beating all at the same time. It observes literally everything around you to make sure that you are safe. You can never, ever overwork your subconscious mind. It's a literal BEAST! However, your conscious mind ain't in the same club. It's in the same body, but it's not in the same club.

Your conscious mind is the one that we need to reign in. *Ahh, the conscious mind. . . . You little scatterbrained gatekeeper you.* The craziest thing to me about the conscious mind is that for some reason it was designed to be the gatekeeper for the beast. Imagine having a jester in control of who gets to see the king. Do that and you will have a good idea about how the conscious mind works.

- ☐ Want to know the one thing that you must do to take control of your conscious mind?

- ☐ Want to know how to make the gatekeeper work for you?

- ☐ Want to know how to trick and eventually control the jester?

You have to overload it with information. You have to only present it with the information that you want it to work on. The only way to do that is to flood it with thoughts and ideas. You need to become a continual learner.

Yup, you gotta flood that motha! Every day your conscious mind wakes up looking for stuff to do. Every minute your conscious mind is looking for trouble to get into, things to think about, problems to solve, and even problems to create.

The Buddha called the conscious mind the monkey mind because it swings from thought to thought. The best way to control your conscious mind is to give it the next thought to swing to. Kind of like training a puppy or, I guess in this case, a monkey mind. Monkey minds, like puppies, have to run and get tired before you can work with them. They have to get all of their energy out.

When you are a continual learner all of the thoughts that your mind swings to are thoughts that you put out there for it to grab onto. Flooding your conscious mind with what you want it to focus on will help you become more of what you want to become. Feed your monkey mind with the information you need to improve your life and your subconscious mind will do the rest. The gatekeeper can't control everything that approaches the gate. That's why you have to make sure that everything that approaches the gate is helpful. Everything that you introduce should be something that pushes you toward your goals.

Most people will allow anyone and everyone to program their minds and, by default, program their life. It's what's been done for centuries. Here's how it works.

The Escapism Trap

People are looking for an escape from their daily life, so what do they do? Most of the time when they get off work, they are exhausted both physically and mentally. They turn on some escapism programming and escape. At least that's what they think that they are doing. The only problem is that they are escaping to someone else's idea of what escapism looks like. (See our earlier story about focus groups.)

The answer is to keep learning. You have to choose what you are going to escape to. You have to chose something that is going to help you reach your full potential. That is the only way to reprogram the years of other people's programming. Most people get their diploma and they never pick up a book again. I mean maybe they read Harry Potter or something, but never anything that is going to improve their life. As much as I love Harry Potter, learning about Hogwarts isn't going to improve your life. That will not be you.

Most people are trying to reach new goals with old information. Most people are trying to improve their lives with old anecdotes from generations long ago. That plan of action leads to a lot of frustration.

Imagine if you stopped learning in middle school and your goal was to be a lawyer. Obviously, that wouldn't work. As a lawyer you have to be constantly studying cases. You have to keep yourself aware of changing laws. That new information could mean your clients' freedom and in the long run it could mean success for your firm.

But right now, we aren't talking about lawyers and firms. Right now, we are talking about your life and filling up your conscious mind with information that will help you get to where you want to go.

Warren Buffett reads six hours a day or 500 pages. The more you read the more capable you become. He also says that knowledge is like compound interest, it builds on itself. Knowledge fills up those thought gaps that we just created by getting rid of old thoughts. As someone who reads about three hours a day (I got kids) I can tell you this: when you read, life on this planet gets super easy. I mean SUPER easy.

As a result of reading and constantly learning I easily raised my credit score after the repossession. I started a business and grew it to multiple six figures. I started a side hustle business and grew it to almost 80k in the first year on top of my other income. I helped my kids reach some of their goals with ease and I'm killing it in my marriage and I'm not special. I'm just a regular guy who reads. Continuous learning is the great cheat code, and the crazy thing is that only a few use it.

No matter how unique you think that your situation is, somebody has had the same or a very similar experience and has found the answer. When you read you just skip to the answer. Do yourself a favor and skip to the answers.

To get you started I linked to a few must reads over on the download. Once you get going you will find yourself continuing down the reading and new information wormhole at lightning speed. You will find your life improving and you will find your stress level dropping. You will find that your overall life will level up. This will include some of your friends and associates so be prepared. No disrespect to the people that you know now, but some of them will not be coming with you to the upgrade part of your journey. As Jim Rohn said,

> *You are the average of the five people you spend the most time with. – Jim Rohn*

It is what it is. More on that and the "The Day Job and The Oscar Winner Story Part 2" In the next chapter.

Your Seventh Assignment

List 5 books on your industry or on your goal that you are going to read.

_____

_____

_____

_____

_____

_____

CHAPTER 8

STEP 8 - YOU ARE THE AVERAGE

Show me your friends and I'll show you your future. –
Unknown

There I was living in Los Angeles. This is pre recorded deal, pre Broadway, and pre any success in music at all. I was your typical starving artist. Literally close to starving. OK well, I'm being dramatic, but you get the idea. At the time I was dating a young lady who I met at work. She and I worked together at the consumer testing place along with her roommate. Basically, like I was saying before, we cold called people and tried to get them in to test products. The people got paid a hundred bucks or so to give their opinion and we got paid to find people to come in and give their opinion. Win-win. Back then the bonus was eating the food that was untouched or left in the testing room. Man in hindsight I can't help but think, WHAT THE HELL WERE

WE THINKING? EATING LEFTOVER FOOD FROM A FOCUS GROUP?" Ah to be young dumb.

As glamorous as it sounds it was like any other job. My then girlfriend, her roommate and I would work all day and complained all night. You know, the usual work for a living kind of deal.

However, on Wednesdays, my girlfriend, her roommate, and I would all have dinner together and watch *South Park*. It was our own little L.A. family away from family tradition. After about a month or two of this, my girlfriend's roommate started missing our dinner/South Park watching get-togethers. She started hanging out with some of her new friends. My girlfriend and I got a little upset about the whole thing and we let her know it. I mean, we had a tradition. You can't start hanging out with other people during our "tradition" time. There were *South Park* episodes to watch for goodness's sake.

Despite our protests she became less and less available for our weekly tradition and more available for these "new friends." After a little bit of our hounding and stuff, she invited us to come and hang with her and her new friends.

According to her, her new friends were getting involved with the industry and she thought they could be a good resource for us as well. I mean, watching *South Park* every Wednesday is a great way to break into the entertainment industry, but this meeting friends who are actually in the industry thing might be something to look into as well.

So we did. One time. Always up to try new things. We didn't like it. There were all these young Hollywood types and they were all caught up in talking about the film industry and stuff. Boring! Yeah, we were stuck on a special kind of stupid back then. Who wants to do something boring like talk about the industry? Psshh! BORING!

Long story even longer, eventually we didn't hang out with her roommate at all. She was gone on this get together and that get together. We were thrown aside. I mean…some people! We went on with our own way of doing things. Obviously, later my girlfriend and I broke up. Her roommate however, went on to win an Oscar. Her roommate was none other than Octavia Spencer. Google her!

I told you that to tell you this. Sometimes your new level of success will require new friends and associates. This is the part of the journey that a lot of people hate. People like to talk about the "Day 1's" and how they stuck with them through everything. However, that is a rare thing. Most of the people that are successful don't have Day 1's still around. (With the exception of your parents or your sisters and brothers. #sometimes) Most of the time you will have to do like Octavia did. Most of the time you are going to have to find new friends that are going the same place you want to go. It's just the way it is.

It's that way because a lot of the time your current friends will unintentionally sabotage your success. How do I know? I know because I was one of those friends. We wanted to keep our unproductive cartoon watching meetings going instead of going out and networking with people in the actual entertainment industry. We were those sabotaging friends. Don't get stuck or left behind because you want to stay true to the old schools. Be sure, no matter what you do going forward, that you stay true to yourself.

I read in some article that said that the idea of being the average of the five people you spend the most time around was untrue. The writer said that he had scientifically proven that that was not the case. Well, I want you to do your own evaluation. Let's begin.

1. Make a list of five of your current closest friends or associates.

2. Ask yourself this question. Are we all about the same income level? Success level? Happiness level? Level level?

If you are like most people, you will probably answer yes. Don't let me put words in your mouth. Do the evaluation for yourself. As Gary Vaynerchuck says in the download you don't have to get rid of all of your friends just get rid of one loser friend. Hey, you can obviously do what you want. It's your life. However, If I were you, I would take the Octavia route and start networking and hanging around people who are looking to level up. You owe you.

Being around new people will be very inspirational and motivational. Their new ideas will inspire you to a new way of thinking. Their presence will motivate you to do better, be better, and have better.

Want to get into your dream life a lot faster? Surround yourself with people who are looking to level up their lives. Put yourself in situations where you are the dumbest in the room.

It doesn't always have to be in person. These days you can do it virtually too. That is the beautiful part of the information age. There are literally no boundaries. Here are some ways that you can network and meet new people who are looking to level up, just in case you need some inspiration.

5 Ways To Connect With People Looking To Level Up!

1. Join a group based on your industry or interest. (Free ones are good, but the level up folks are usually in the paid ones.)

2. Listen to podcasts based on your interests or goals. (These are always free, but if they offer a paid program or online course that is going to be where the connections will happen.)

3. Follow influencers in your industry on social media. (Lots of information to be learned out there and they will share it with you.)

4. Go to conventions and events that are in your niche or topic of interest.

5. Read books! (The information in these things is priceless and can also connect you with people, places, and things that can help you level up and get those old thoughts out of your head.)

No matter what anyone says, you definitely are the average of the five people you spend the most time with. If you like your average, then don't change a thing. However, if you want more you are going to have to change a lot. There is no right or wrong answer. It's your choice, but the truth will remain the same. As Zig Ziglar says . . .

"You become part of what you are around." – Zig Ziglar

Well, if you have been counting (Or reading the chapter titles) you know that this was the final secret of the eight. Nice work if you were paying attention. However, like everything in life there is always more.

Before I let you go, I wanted to share three bonus myths or old ideals that tripped me up along the way. My hope is that by sharing them you can avoid being tripped up by them as well. On to the bonus sections my friend! We've got some myth busting to do!

Your Eighth Assignment

List 5 organizations in person or virtual that you are going to join.

_____

_____

_____

_____

_____

List 3 organizations that you are going to join in your community.

_____

_____

_____

_____

_____

CHAPTER 9

THE HARD WORK MYTH

There I was, an O.G.-style entrepreneur working my tail off. I was doing the fourteen to sixteen hour days, plopped in front of my laptop, skipping sleep, and doing the eating on the go thing. Like most people, that is what I thought was needed to be successful. The "Grind Till You Die" motto is everywhere on the internet and I had bought in. Whelp, I am here to tell you that is wrong. That was and is an outdated belief and I was the one who had to decide to get rid of it.

Now I am not saying that you will not have to work your ass off to get the results that you want to have, but I am saying that it is not the goal full stop. The goal is to get to the goal. For instance, now that Jeff Bezos has set Amazon up to be one of the largest if not the largest retailer in the world you can find him sailing around the world and enjoying life. The goal is not to work until you die. The goal is to work so that you can live.

The next step in this process is getting rid of old outdated beliefs. Now, don't be surprised if you get triggered when you start to hear stuff like this. That's what happened when I started telling people that never ending hard work was *not* the key to success.

When I started challenging the "grind till you die" culture they freaked out and, to be honest, until the new way started working for me so did I. It will be the same for you. Showing, however, is better than telling. Let them see the results when you get done. That will take out all of the fruitless debating and point proving that comes with new thoughts and beliefs.

Just a point of reference. I started a business during the pandemic. It's a 100% digital passive income business. It is about one year old and it is already on pace to pass the income that some of my other businesses are generating. Here's the real kicker. I literally only need to work about an hour or so a day to maintain it and about three or four hours a day to grow it.

Did I work hard for the first year? Yes! But after a year I am about to see a lifestyle of ongoing growing income that will require less and less of my time. As Leon

Howard, aka the Wallstreet Trapper says, a lot of us know a lot of people with two and three jobs who are broke. Hard work isn't the goal. Time freedom and life experience is.

"Hard work won't get you everywhere you wanna be at!"

Leon Howard (The Wallstreet Trapper)

As he says, he was working on a construction site when he realized that he was working hard but not heading toward the goal of financial freedom. He said:

"Think about this, on a job, the person who works the hardest gets paid the least. The person who gets paid the most is the person who has to think the most. He has a different type of information. So, I was building the Falcon stadium. Right?! So, I was getting paid about 41 dollars an hour. I was doing the hard work. Putting the harness on everyday that's about fifty pounds. I gotta climb forty feet in the air and then get up there and do more work."

He went on to say, and I'm paraphrasing right now:

"My foreman didn't have to climb that high. He's getting paid about 60 dollars an hour. His boss was at the front of the site in the air conditioned "can" telling us what we

150

needed to do. He was making about 80 dollars an hour. The person who was over him actually owns the business isn't even at the site. He's making a million every project. Do you see what I mean?"

Hard work is a part of the solution. However, it's not the whole solution.

I tell you that to tell you this. Understanding that the answer full stop isn't just hard work is a gift. Getting rid of that old belief and old beliefs like it is going to save you years of frustration and struggle. As it relates to hard work; you have to know that finding the smart way and then working hard is going to be the most helpful thing going forward.

Don't go around pushing on doors that say pull. Hard work is a means, but it definitely is not the end. As you work hard, you'll need to learn to step back, evaluate your situation, see if the door says pull on it, see if it's even the right door, see if someone around you has a key, and so on and so forth. Are we clear?

So where did the idea of hard work come from? I am a fan of learning the history of things. It helps you see how relevant or irrelevant a belief might be these days. For instance, working hard and never stopping is a very Protestant ideal. Back when they thought of this whole idea, those folks were racing against the seasons. That way of thinking was super necessary for those European settlers back then.

They were on land that they didn't know, trying to make sure that they didn't die. They had to grow food on a terrain that was very unfamiliar to them. Plus, they all knew that there had been a lot of other settlers who had died as a result of not getting this "how to get food" thing right. So, they had to grind in order not to die. That's not your reality my friend.

You are more like the American Indians. They didn't have to work so hard. They had information. They knew the land. They knew where to move to when the seasons changed. They understood the land so they could relax a little bit more. Did they work hard? Of course they did! But they didn't have to grind like the European settlers. They had information.

You have information! You can literally walk to get food if you had to. You can literally go on the internet and find great opportunities. That was then and this is now. Be a user of information. Information is the new currency.

The settlers didn't have computers back then. They didn't have cars back then. They didn't have the internet back then. That being said, they might not be the best people to turn to in a day and age where you can make a living selling digital things that you can create one time.

But you know us humans. We keep saying and believing things despite how outdated they are. We are still in love with old ideas from hundreds of years ago. Just something to think about. After Amazon took off Jeff Bezos just left Amazon as chief executive. He's doing it right.

Hard work is necessary, don't get me wrong, but it's not the full answer.

Change Your Thoughts, Change Your LIFE!

One more reference that proves that information is better than perspiration. Ray Kroc wasn't flipping burgers at the McDonald's on the weekends for the restaurants he franchised. Do you know who was? The McDonald's brothers. They were doing what the old settlers thought was a good thing to do. They were doing all of the hard work.

Ray Kroc came along, not having worked in a hamburger joint EVAH, and systemized the whole kit and kaboodle. Eventually he sold the McDonald's brother's business to the world. Ray turned McDonald's into the global giant that we know today. I repeat! He didn't even work in the hamburger business. He used his knowledge and information and hired people to work a system that he embellished for the business based on what he saw the McDonald's brothers doing. He didn't even create the system. We all know how that turned out. Bill Gates isn't down at the production plant assembling computers.

Don't hate the player, LEARN the game!

Hard work won't get you there!

There I was, a Broadway star in the Broadway show RENT! By all accounts I had "made it!" I was doing a show on Broadway making six figures a year doing music. I was good right? Wrong. When the student is ready the teacher will appear. That was the first time that I learned that my programming was wrong. I had been doing the show for six months and my contract was up for renewal. Of course, I was going to renew. I had made it, right?!? I was making some paper doing what I love! Let's go!

Well, one day after a performance the producers of the show came backstage to make an announcement. It was a big deal. Everyone was called into the greenroom. It was actually a mandatory meeting which kind of stressed me out because I had to catch the last New Jersey transit bus in order to make it home and there wasn't much time between the end of the show and the last bus. On top of that, New Jersey transit bus drivers don't play. When the bus driver closed the door that was it. If you weren't on the bus, you ain't getting on the bus. Be late at your own expense. I've seen a dude run up to the door as it was closing only to be left at that station. One time a lady did that and got mad and started banging on the door. The bus driver called over the cops, she got a ticket, and still had to find another way home. It's real out there in New York.

Anyway, the producers had come to watch the show that night. After the show they came into the greenroom in their black New York overcoats and stuff to make their big announcement. Adam Pascal and Anthony Rapp were coming back to do the show. It was going to bring a buzz to the show and sell more tickets. For those of you who aren't familiar with RENT, Adam and Anthony were the original cast members and to have them back was going to make the fans go crazy!

There were cheers all around the room (that is, from everyone except for the two cast members that they would be replacing). Everyone was invited next door for a private after-party. I am not one for partying. Plus, I was trying to get on that last bus. As you now know, them bus drivers don't play and that was my only way home. On my way out of the theater I walked past one of the producers and he asked if I was going to the party. I said, "No, I gotta go home. My wife waits up for me and besides that, the last bus runs in about five minutes."

This man looked at me and said something like, "At least stop by and have a drink. We bought the bar and we got it catered. Hey, I'll pay for you to get a cab home." Wait WHUUUT! I thought.

Keep in mind. I lived in Montclair, New Jersey, and we were in Manhattan. When I told him that I lived in New Jersey he didn't even bat an eye. He said, "No problem," reached into his jacket pocket, and pulled out a fat roll of one-hundred-dollar bills, peeled off three of them and handed them to me. "This will cover your cab," he said. "Go and have a drink."

That brother was walking around with a roll of hunnits in his pockets. Like a real roll held together with a rubber band. It was some gansta New York shit. I had never seen anything like it before in my life. If that wasn't a lesson in it takes more than hard work, I don't know what would be. There I was working hard, doing eight shows a week with one day off and this man who I had NEVER SEEN BEFORE IN MY LIFE was the one really achieving success. I knew right then that I was on the wrong side of this equation. My mind started to race! How many shows was he producing?

The whole ride home, all I could think about were these facts:

1. I had worked there for five months and up until that point and I had never seen that man before in my life, yet he was the producer of the show and making real bank.

2. He was making enough money to pay all of our salaries, plus the band, the owner of the building, and everything else and still have a roll of hundreds in his pocket that he treated like spare change.

3. He never had to do a show ever, yet he made more money than all of us combined.

Eyes opened! Leon the Wallstreet Trapper is right! I think that the only person I know of that has two or three jobs and is super successful is Steve Harvey, but check this out.

Somewhere in his life is a producer like the one that I met that day. Somebody cuts him a check. They aren't down at the studio everyday filming shows, they are not down at the radio station doing the "special broadcasts." They are at home with their family. They are going to kids or grandkids basketball games.

Now, again, before we wrap this chapter up, I'm NOT telling you that you won't have to work hard. What I am telling you is that working hard cannot and should not be the goal. Working smart should be.

The end results of working hard should mean that there is an exit strategy. The smarter you work the sooner your exit strategy should be. The smart realize that working hard is good in the beginning, but it is a fool's errand to have that be the only objective.

Examples like this are why I say that every belief should be questioned and tested using the information that you have now. Every little bit of programming should be challenged! If your old beliefs don't pass the tests of facts, physical verifiable truth, life experience, or the new information test, they need to be thrown out. That being said, this next section is going to ruffle some feathers, but that's why we're here. To challenge old beliefs. Here we go.

A College Degree Isn't The Only Way...

Mark Zuckerberg, Bill Gates, and Steve Jobs all dropped out of college.

As a matter of fact, *The Wall Street Journal* did an article about this very idea. In the article they talked about how kids were feeling lost. The writer said that a larger number of kids were opting for not enrolling in college because they didn't see it as a viable option anymore.

I was one of those kids who put two and two together and realized that college was not for me. I was a freshman at college and one of the school's superstars was graduating that year. This guy was a college god to me. He was praised by staff, he was a super musician, and he was even allowed to conduct the choir and the orchestra when the professors wanted to show him off. Nobody else was allowed to do that. Well, one of the professors' kids did it, but that felt more like a nepotism deal than a merit-based deal. Anyways. . .

Later that year he graduated, and everyone went on with life and school and stuff. That was, until my junior year. There I was in the halls of the music building and there he was, the music god of my freshman year. I was shocked. "What are you doing here?" I asked him. Turns out that despite being one of the best musicians I had ever known and despite having a college degree and all of the things that they say that you should have, he couldn't get a job working as a musician. He had a music degree and couldn't get a job as a music teacher!

That was my *aha* moment. I dropped out of college after that year and still have not returned to college and have no plans to. I'm doing alright and I'm doing it without the thing that everyone said was the key to success.

Another old idea that jacked me up was the old idea that if you put out good energy good things will come to you. Well, Martin Luther King and Medgar Evers were assassinated, so there's that. Plus, during the same time in America four little girls were killed by a bomb at the 16th street Baptist church. I think people would be hard-pressed to find the stream of bad energy that those little kids put out into the world.

Look, counter to popular belief, the world is made up of good and bad. You are going to have to deal with both.

When you are dealing with what IS instead of what you want to be, you will have the advantage over everyone. Kind of like when you realized that Santa wasn't coming and that if you wanted to have presents under the Christmas tree you were going to have to buy them and put them under the dang thang yourself.

When it comes to life, some people are still waiting for Santa Claus to bring them their goals and dreams. Don't be one of those adults waiting for Santa. I've seen the results and it doesn't end well.

Did you know the top regret of the dying is that they didn't live the life that they wanted to live? That's deep! You live the life that you want to live by challenging and moving out old beliefs that aren't serving you.

Challenge your old beliefs. Keep the ones that can withstand the challenge and throw out the rest.

"But Wait, There's More!"

CHAPTER 10

THE UNREALISTIC GOALS MYTH

I magine being a little girl living in extreme poverty and telling your friends that you are going to be one of the wealthiest women in the world. Imagine telling those same friends that people all over the globe are going to watch you on television one day and that just by putting a book on your book club list you are going to be able to make it a New York Times Bestseller.

What do you think your friends would have told you? They would have probably told you all the things that your friends are telling you now about your "unrealistic goals". You know...sounds something like this.

- You're gonna do what?

- Make sure that you have a fall-back plan.

- That's a good goal, but....

You know the usual "have realistic goals" chorus. Had she listened to those friends like so many people do, the world would have never known Oprah Winfrey. Even after she had pushed past all those obstacles, the world of doubting Thomas' was still out in full force. A producer for the news station that she was working at told her that she was "unfit for television."

Only you know what you are called to do. Other people will get it wrong 99.9% of the time. Be like Oprah. Dream big, write your goals down, and keep traveling toward your "unrealistic" destination. It's only unrealistic for the caterpillars. I said what I said.

Imagine that you were this weird kid who was always getting into trouble and causing mischief. Imagine that people pegged your rebellious outbreaks to you being adopted and not really being OK with it. Then imagine that your father is a machinist who didn't graduate high school and your mom is an accountant and they know nothing about your biggest interest. Plus, they don't really have the financial resources to even support a path into that new aged digital world of computers. Now imagine telling your friends that you are going to start a company in your parent's garage that will rival IBM. If the person that I'm talking about would have listened to their laughs and words of discouragement, the world would have never had Apple computers or Steve Jobs.

Now imagine being a kid who was born on the floor in an abandoned building in 1945. Then imagine being labeled educable mentally retarded by your teachers. Then imagine telling your friends that one day you are going to marry Gladys Knight, become a member of the Ohio House of Representatives, and become one of the leading motivational speakers of all time. If this person would have listened to the howls and laughs of his friends, we would have never known Les Brown.

The list goes on and on and on. How about growing up in the projects (JAY-Z), or how about losing your mom, not having a dad since you were eight years old, and still going on to become a multi-platinum artist, a television producer and businessman of multiple seven figure companies (50 Cent). How about growing up in the deep south in the 40s, being molested as a child and not speaking for years because of it, and still becoming a film actor, a world-renowned author, and even having your face minted on a coin (Maya Angelou).

Imagine what those conversations would be like, trying to tell the people around you about your goals. Yeah, unrealistic goals are only unrealistic because people share them with people who have a limited understanding of life and what we as human beings are really capable of.

Remember what we talked about before. Keep your dreams to yourself. As one of my favorite sayings goes,

"No one is supposed to understand your calling, it wasn't a conference call."

Make your goals extremely unreasonable and keep them private. Here is what I would suggest that you do for yourself. Take all of your unreasonable goals and make them your midway goals. I want you to make your final goals the ones that people say are super ridiculously unrealistic. I want you to dream bigger than you ever have before. That big unrealistic dream is actually more realistic than you think.

The problem that most people have is that we don't know what we don't know. We can't see what we can't see. Remember the whole "you are the average of the people that hang around?" Well, know that you can change that by raising your goals and then by moving in different circles. See the Octavia Spencer story. I lived that one personally. Learn from my mistakes.

So how do you make the leap when you don't know how?

Here's what you do. Well, let me rephrase. Here's what I did. I'm still on my way to my next big goal, but hopefully this will help you see that it can work.

So here it is.

Step 1: Take your unreasonable unrealistic goal and make it your middle goal.

No matter what your goals are right now, I can guarantee that they are too small. All of our goals are My goal of reaching 1 million dollars this calendar year is probably too small too. Like I said before, we don't know what we don't know, and we can't see what we can't see. The first step is to realize that there are possibilities that are available to you that you don't even know are available to you. The first time I passed 300,000 a year my goal was 100k. You don't know what you don't know. I shot past my goal, and to most of the people that I knew, even the first goal was unrealistic for a new business.

As a matter of fact, one of the people closest to me told me as much.

So, take your goal and make it your middle goal and then take that unrealistic goal and make it your end goal.

Step 2: The work that you planned on doing and multiply it by 10.

Hopefully you're noticing a theme. The theme is that at minimum you are operating on a tenth of your potential. Einstein once said that we are basically operating on 10% of our overall brain's capacity. Based on what I've seen, it's the same with life. At maximum we are going through life working at 10% of your ability. Even making it to a 50% would be five times what you are doing right now.

Imagine a life where everything that you experience is five times better than it is now. How amazing would your life be? Well, in order to get there, we can't just "make a wish and then go and eat a sandwich," as Jim Carey says. We have to do some work and that usually means about ten times the work that you have been doing. The beautiful part is that the work that you have been doing is only about 10% of what you're capable of doing. You can do this!

Step 3: Work Smarter AND Harder!

We talked about this earlier in the book but pushing on a door that says pull isn't going to work. I know that we got a grind culture floating around out there, but that's why most people are burned out and always falling short of their goals. Working hard isn't enough. I told you that earlier in this book too. Always be evaluating. Always be shifting. Always be adjusting for maximum success.

Airplanes make thousands of adjustments on their way toward their destination. When you walk down the street you are making thousands of little adjustments just to walk. Your brain is adjusting for balance. It's adjusting for the different height levels of the ground below you, it's adjusting for the wind, the movement of the planet, the person walking toward you.

Your subconscious mind is constantly making thousands of little adjustments to help you reach your success. Your subconscious mind already knows that working smart and hard are super important. Follow its lead.

You have to be willing to adjust to reach your goal. It's crazy out here in these streets. Work harder and smarter and be willing to make adjustments. Don't let failure derail you. It's a part of the process. Keep going! With each failure you are getting smarter. With each failure you are learning one more way that will not work. Eventually you will run out of ways that won't work and only have ways that will work. Keep going!

Finally, I want to give you one last thing to think about and that is stealing.

CHAPTER 11

STEALING IS BAD MYTH

"Good artists borrow. Great artists steal!" – Pablo
Picasso

I f you are smart you will steal everything that you can and put your spin on it. If you are smart. Look, someone already figured out everything that you want to do. There are a lot of people who already had amazing success at the exact goal that you are trying to reach. Just take what they did, add your little touch, and apply what worked for them to your life.

Kobe Bryant copied Michael Jordan. Everyone knew what he was doing including Michael. He literally mimicked everything about that man and because of it he won five titles, one shy of Jordan. I know we dismiss copying as some kind of shortfall, but five titles is five titles. That is the power of copying.

Bruce Lee copied the fighters that came before him and so did Mike Tyson. Based on the quote, Picasso copied too. Elvis stole from Big Mama Thornton; Gretzky stole from Gordie Howe, Madam C.J. Walker stole from Annie Malone. Speaking of Madam C.J. Walker and unrealistic goals, her parents were former slaves. Despite her parents being owned by someone and despite living in the late 1800s, she became a millionaire. Look, steal everything and put your spin on it. Don't try to be the original schmiginal. That is dumb.

Even for those people who we call "the original" there is someone who has done exactly what they are trying to do in some way, shape, or form. We just don't know about them. There is a saying that goes, "There is nothing new under the sun!" and it basically means that everything that can be done has been done.

So don't think of this as a call to challenge that idea. Think of this as a call to find out who the person is that you are supposed to be copying. Your job is to figure out how you are going to put your spin on it. Do that!

Literally every success that I have had has come on the heels of copying someone. When I was auditioning for RENT I copied Jesse, the original Collins in RENT.

All of the guys that were auditioning ahead of me were trying to be the original schmiginal. They were doing all of these runs and vocal acrobatics that a singer could do. I was literally no match for them vocally. However, I remember hearing the casting director say, "Can you make it more believable? I want to feel like you lost a loved one." (See stepping back and evaluating the situation. They were working hard and I was working smart.)

He said those words to singer after singer. To me that was basically him saying, "We don't need all of that original schmiginal stuff. We need someone who can do what Jesse did because that worked. That made our show a hit." Do you know what ya boi did? He copied and then he got the job.

Copy and copy some more. Steal and steal some more. It really is that simple and as the saying goes . . .

"K.I.S.S. Keep it simple, stupid."

CHAPTER 12

THE FINAL WORD

Well, you have done something that most people don't do. You made it to the end of the book. Congratulations my friend. You are already ahead of the crowd. No but seriously, congratulations and good job! You are already elite.

Now, I don't want to beat a dead horse, but I do want to make sure that you get a brief refresher before you go off into the world of constant interruptions and distractions.

You now have the tools to not only get out of your own head, but to make sure that the space inside of your head is a place where your dreams are allowed to flourish into your new reality.

Don't pass up this opportunity and don't miss your chance to get your free download over at thisiswhereitallends.com It's still free and it has a lot of great bonus material just waiting for you! Now, let's make sure that you remember all of the things that we talked about in this book. You owe it to yourself. Here are the unconventional steps one more time.

Step 1: Take Responsibility For Everything!

Start today! Taking responsibility for everything is a game changer. Now remember, this doesn't mean that you have to go around declaring it to the world. This can be a you thing. As a matter of fact, it should be a you thing.

If things go bad. You are responsible. If things go well. You are responsible. If things are just average. You are responsible. Take responsibility for everything that happens in your life.

Step 2: Talk To Yourself Like You're All You Got Because You're All You Got.

Start talking to yourself like you are your best friend. Stop saying negative things to yourself about yourself. Start speaking your goals into existence. Start challenging any negative words that you say to yourself. Make sure that you change all of that negative talk to positive talk. That will show you that you have got your back.

Step 3. Stop Being An HTH.

Stop being a Head Trash Hoarder. Most of the limiting beliefs that affect your day to day aren't even your beliefs. Someone else put those in your mind. You were a kid and so you held on to them, but you aren't a kid anymore. You are responsible for your life. Don't be a head trash hoarder. Get rid of all those trash thoughts that are holding you back. Have your own Saturday Gospel cleanout and put them in your own mental file 13. Ya' Welcome!

Step 4: The Mentor Factor.

Get a mentor that knows your story. You owe it to yourself to have a mentor in your mentor tribe that knows your life experience. If you are a woman, you should have at least one woman in your mentor group. If you are a man, you should have at least one man in your mentor group. If you are Latin, Black, Asian, or whatever you should have at minimum one mentor that knows your experience. You owe it to yourself. Get a mentor in your group of mentors who knows your story from an "I lived it" point of view.

Step 5: Stop The Flow.

Your media, music, and entertainment are shaping your reality. Those images are telling you what is important and what is impossible. They are telling you what love looks like and what happiness looks like. They are telling you what failure looks like and what success looks like and more than likely some rando from off the street is the one responsible for your programming.

You are allowing someone or in many cases a group of someones who don't even know you to program you. You are letting total strangers dictate your life. Take control of your life. Turn off anything that isn't helping you reach YOUR ideals of success, happiness, and love and turn on only the things that are helping you achieve those goals. Become your own reality programmer.

Now this will mean that you will have days and maybe even weeks where you will have no entertainment to watch or listen to. So, turn on some fun educational audiobook or documentary or something. Take over your own programming and stop the negative flow.

Step 6: Manifestation Creation Guide.

Don't make this harder than it needs to be. Speak it. Write it. Then move on and do it. How's that for straight to the point.

Step 7: No Summer School.

Never ever ever ever stop learning. Fill your head with not only specific knowledge but random knowledge about the goals and dreams that you are looking to reach. Become a student of whatever niche, industry or topic, you are looking to be successful in. Be obsessed!

Like we talked about in the earlier chapters, Warren Buffet reads five hours a day and you can bet he's not rereading Harry Potter. He's reading stuff that has to do with his goals. I can guarantee that! Be like Warren!

Step 8: You Are The Average.

If nine of your friends are broke, you are going to be number ten. It's just the way it is. If you want to have a different life, you are going to have to add or in many cases change the people that you hang around.

Look, this stuff isn't always feel goody and cute, but neither is dying with regret. That stuff really ain't cute.

Seen it firsthand and trust me, you don't want that. Raise your average by surrounding yourself with people who are going where you want to go. If you want to really raise your average, surround yourself with people who are already where you want to go. That's the real flex.

Well, that's all I got my friend. I really hope that you use the information that you have. I myself have been guilty of knowing something and not applying it. This is your time to apply. It does you no good to just know it. Just knowing things doesn't change your life. Applying those things does. Go and do!

You now have everything that you need to make the shift. The rest is up to you.

The last question is, will you do what you need to do to make sure that "this is ACTUALLY where it all ends" and also that "this is where your new life begins"? Only you can answer that question! You have the tools. Now you have to decide if you will use them. You're up!

I want to leave you with one last story. My hope in telling you this story is that it motivates you to live your life to the absolute fullest. These two situations were life changing for me and I want to share them with you because that is what my parents would have wanted.

I was in the room when my mom died. It was just her and I. I actually saw her take her last breath. Seeing that will change your life. Even in that moment she was teaching me. She was teaching me that you can do a lot of things for a lot of people. You can serve the masses and your family. You can be everyone's idea of a strong person. You can be everyone's hero. No matter what you are or who you think you are or who other people think that you are you are going to the great beyond by yourself. Nobody is coming with you. You better get right with yourself. You had better make sure that you are good with you because you are literally all you got.

I didn't get to be in the room when my dad died. I was actually on a plane and had just left him a couple of days before I got the call. Before his last days he said to me, "Son, when I get out of here, I am going to drive all across the country. I'm going to get involved with some groups and meet some new people. When I get out of here, I'm going to do a lot of the stuff that I have been thinking about."

The problem was that he was already in hospice care. He wasn't getting out. In that moment he taught me that waiting is truly a misconception. We act like we have unlimited amounts of time when none of us knows when our time is going to be up. In that moment he taught me to stop waiting. Whatever you want to do you need to do it now because now is all that you really have.

I wanted to share those lessons with you because a lot of times people pick up a book and read it and then put it down and pick up a new one. I get it. I do it! However, this time I want you to make sure that you apply this stuff to your life. You deserve to live the life of your dreams. You deserve to live life to the fullest. My hope in sharing those stories is that this will be one more push to inspire you to do that now. Not tomorrow. Not the next day. Not when everything gets all in a row. NOW! Do it NOW!

Stay awesome my friend and remember that I am truly cheering for you. I want you to win and win big.

In closing, thank you for allowing me to be a small part of your journey. Thank you for spending some of your time with me. I hope that it has been helpful, and I pray that it has been a blessing. I look forward to hearing about your success. See you in the Awesome Life Hall of Fame!

About The Author

Dad/Musician/Entrepreneur Troy Horne has always wanted to help others achieve their goals. After setting out to become a professional musician Troy starred on Star Search in high school. He was able to get a full scholarship to college however, as you read he dropped out when he saw that it wasn't going to help him reach his goal of becoming a professional musician.

After taking the big leap and moving to Los Angeles, Troy signed a record deal that had him opening for The Steve Miller Band all across the United States. After that he traveled the world with the world-renowned House Jacks touring in Asia and Europe. Then he starred in the Broadway Show RENT as Tom Collins. He played Tom

Collins on Broadway for about a year and then set off to become an entrepreneur.

After his stint on Broadway, he found himself tinkering with music just a little more on The Sing Off on NBC as a part of the group Urban Method. Finally, he went all in on entrepreneurship and ended up taking his business to multiple six figures. In addition to his main business he is using the goal setting techniques that he writes about he was able to take his side hustle to six figures as well.

He has used the things in this book to help improve his marriage, his relationship with his children and most importantly his relationship with self. Inner peace is the assignment! He looks forward to hearing what you will do with them.

"Thank you for allowing me to be a small part of your journey! I super appreciate you and look forward to hearing your story of success." - Troy Horne

Other Books By The Author

Other books that troy has written include:

First Time Dad - An Expectant Father's Weekly Guide To Pregnancy

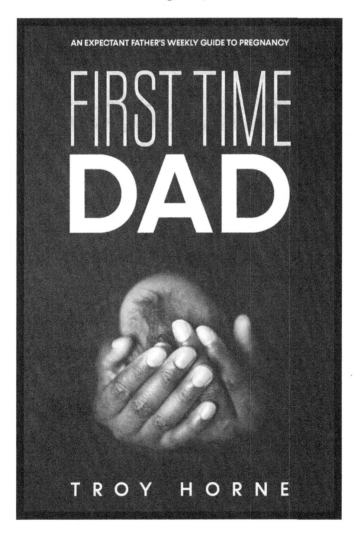

FINAL NOTES AND BONUSES!

If you enjoyed the book please don't forget to leave a review!

Just Click here!

Or visit!

https://amzn.to/38H2f8E

Those things are absolute gold and help me help more people. I can't tell you enough how grateful I will be for your honest review.

Just click the link and do your thing. Thank you again for allowing me to be a part of your journey.

Also, don't forget to pick up your free bonus download at thisiswhereitallends.com

Thank you!

Made in the USA
Coppell, TX
19 May 2022

77946116R00114